Frederick H Fisher

Afghanistan and the Central Asian Question

Frederick H Fisher

Afghanistan and the Central Asian Question

ISBN/EAN: 9783744753456

Printed in Europe, USA, Canada, Australia, Japan

Cover: Foto ©ninafisch / pixelio.de

More available books at **www.hansebooks.com**

AFGHANISTAN

AND

THE CENTRAL ASIAN QUESTION.

BY

FRED. H. FISHER,

B.A. LOND., OF THE MIDDLE TEMPLE, AND H.M. BENGAL CIVIL SERVICE;

Author of "Cyprus, our New Colony, and what we know about it."

WITH MAP.

London:
JAMES CLARKE & CO., 13 & 14, FLEET STREET, E.C.
—
1878.

"For my own part, I will only say that though I should have preferred, in the interest of peace, that Russia had not entered on a career of conquest along the Jaxartes and the Oxus, yet I see no reason at present to feel any anxiety about the advance towards India. Asia is large enough for both of us, and we may well pursue our respective paths, and fulfil our respective missions, without jostling or jealousy. Our position in Asia is quiescent, while hers is progressive. . . . We can, therefore, well afford to wait, forbearing, but vigilant, and conscious that if real danger approaches at any time, we are strong enough to arrest and crush it."—SIR HENRY RAWLINSON'S "Notes on Khiva," *March, 1873.*

PREFACE.

THE author's best apology for the present book must be the absence of any single English work, so far, at least, as he knows, which professes to give a comprehensive account of the land of the Afghans, the people, and their history, including all that is most important in the past, as well as the more immediately interesting subject of the present, relations of Afghanistan with Great Britain. If the following pages in any way carry out the above idea of what is required at the present juncture of affairs on our Indian frontier, the author's object will have been accomplished. It remains to him to acknowledge the very great obligations under which he lies to the authors and publications named on a subsequent page, besides many that have escaped mention. One subject of regret the author has had in connection with this work. He had hoped to have been able himself to see it through the press; but, having to return to duty in India rather more suddenly than he had expected, he has had to leave the task of revising the proof-sheets to a friend, to whose kindness in undertaking it the author is deeply indebted.

FRED. H. FISHER.

P.S.—It was originally intended to have a map prepared especially for this volume, but the excellent map published by Messrs. George Philip and Son, of Fleet Street, having since appeared, it has been decided by the publishers to supply it for the use of the readers of this volume. The only drawback to its adoption for this purpose is that the spelling of some of the names of places differs somewhat from the author's. The orthography used in this volume is that which has now obtained almost universal currency, being employed by Sir Henry Rawlinson and other acknowledged masters of Indian subjects. In this system a few names that have acquired a prescriptive title to a conventional (although inaccurate) mode of spelling retain the conventional form, such as Cabul, Candahar, Calcutta, Delhi, &c. Other names are spelt according to Sir William Jones' now well-known method of transliteration. The accentuation, however, has been omitted, as it gives an awkward look to names, and is of very little practical use. To diminish any inconvenience that may arise from having different modes of spelling in the letterpress and the map, a list of the more important names that are spelt differently in them is appended.

PUBLISHERS' NOTE.

From several passages which occur in the latter portion, it will be seen that this work was written previous to the recent publication of the Official Correspondence on Afghan Affairs. The foregoing Preface will explain why these have remained as written.

LIST OF SOME NAMES OF PLACES SPELT DIFFERENTLY IN MAP AND LETTERPRESS.

In Letterpress.	In Map.	Pronounced.
Andkhui	Andkhooi	Andkhōō-i
Bannu	Bunnoo	Bùnnoo
Bhawalpur	Bahawulpore	Bahà (or Bhà) wulpoor
Cabul	Kabool	Càwbul
Candahar	Kandahar	Càndahar
Ghazni	Ghuznee	Ghùznee
Hari Rud	Heri Rud	Hùree Rood
Hindu Kush	Hindoo Koosh	Hìndoo Koosh
Jalalabad	Jelalabad	Jelàlabad
Kala-i-Ghilzai	Kelat-i-Ghiljie	Kàla-i-Ghìlzai
Karachi	Kurrachee	Kooràchee
Khaibar	Khyber	Khỳber
Merv	Merve	Merv
Multan	Mooltan	Mooltàn
Nushki	Nooshky	Noòshkee
Peshawar	Peshawur	Peshàwar
Pishni	Pisheen	Pishnee or Pisheen
Sarakhs	Serakhs	Serùkhs

b

AUTHORITIES.

Sir Jno. Kaye's "History of the War in Afghanistan."
Sir Henry Rawlinson's "England and Russia in the East."
Dr. Bellew's "Journal of a Mission to Afghanistan," "From the Indus to the Tigris," and "Kashmir and Kashgar."
Forster's "Journey from Bengal to England."
Vambery's "Travels."
Burne's   Ditto.
Ferrier's "Caravan Journeys."
Wood's "Journeys."
Captain Havelock's "Narrative."
Stocqueler's "Memorials of Afghanistan."
Philip Smith's "Ancient History."
Meadowes Taylor's "History of India."
Elphinstone's "History of India."
"Encyclopedia Britannica" (Ninth Edition), Articles on "Afghanistan" and "Afghan Turkestan."
English Cyclopedia, Article on "Afghanistan."
Numerous Articles in the "Times," "Pall Mall Gazette," and other Newspapers have been made use of for the Account of more recent Events.

CONTENTS.

CHAPTER I.
AFGHANISTAN—ITS NATURAL FEATURES.

Natural Boundaries—Approximate Extent of Afghanistan—Origin of Name—Independent Territory—What Afghan Dominions Include—Comparison of Afghanistan with Switzerland—Mountain-ranges—Hindu Kush and its Prolongations—Safed Koh—Suliman Mountains—Passes on the Indo-Afghan Frontier—Fort of Ali Musjid—Natural Divisions—Rivers—Lakes—Provinces and Towns . . 1

CHAPTER II.
AFGHANISTAN—ITS CLIMATE AND PRODUCTIONS.

Variations in Climate—Mineral Wealth—Vegetable Kingdom—Agriculture—Irrigation—Animal Kingdom—Domestic Animals—Industry and Commerce—Trade Routes—Povindahs . . . 47

CHAPTER III.
THE PEOPLE, LANGUAGE, LITERATURE, AND ANTIQUITIES OF AFGHANISTAN.

The Afghans, Pathans, or Pushtanahs—Division into Tribes—Non-Afghan Population—Estimated Population—Russian Account—Supposed Jewish Origin—Kafirs—Sir John Kaye's Description of the Afghans—Language and Literature—Judicial Institutions—Military System—Russian Account of the Afghan Army—Antiquities 66

xiv   *Contents.*

CHAPTER IV.
ALEXANDER THE GREAT'S MARCH THROUGH AFGHANISTAN ON INDIA.

                                                                     PAGE

Alexander's Army—Pursuit of Darius after the Battle of Arbela—Conquest of Parthia and Hyrcania—Founding of Herat—Conquest of North-Eastern Afghanistan—Campaign in Bactria—Alexander an Oriental Potentate—Marriage with Roxana—Crosses the Hindu Kush into India—Campaign in India—Voyage of Nearchus from the Indus to the Euphrates—Alexander's March across the Desert of Baluchistan—Greek Influence on the Oxus . 96

CHAPTER V.
AFGHAN HISTORY FROM MUHAMMAD TO ZAMAN SHAH.

First Appearance of Afghanistan in Mediæval History—Arab Settlements—Story of Kasim and the Rajput Princess—The Ghazni Monarchy Founded by Alptagin—Invasion of India—Peshawar the First Permanent Muhammadan Conquest in India—Sabaktagin—Plunder of Somnath—Mahmud of Ghazni—Shahabuddin—Jengis Khan—Timur or Tamerlane Invades Northern India—Babar Founds the Mughal Empire of Irdia—Nadir Shah Invades and Plunders the Panjab—Ahmad Shah Founds the Durani Empire of Afghanistan—Invades India—Battle of Panipat—Zaman Shah—Threatens to Invade India 106

CHAPTER VI.
AFGHAN HISTORY FROM ZAMAN SHAH TO THE EVE OF THE FIRST AFGHAN WAR.

Zaman Shah Advances to Lahore—Panic in British India—Review of Situation — Native Feeling in India — Incidents of Former Invasions — Alarm at French Intrigues — First Symptoms of "Russophobia"—Encroachment of Russia on Persia—Scheme of Joint Russian and French Invasion of India—Sir John Kaye on the Two Classes of Governor-General — Lords Minto and Wellesley Compared with Lord Lytton—The Rise of the Sikhs

—British and Russian Advance Compared—Mission to the Sikhs
—Shah Suja—Rise of the Barakzais—Shah Suja an Exile—Affairs
in Afghanistan before the First Afghan War—Mission of Captain
Burnes and Siege of Herat—Eldred Pottinger—Dost Muhammad
—Sikhs Gain Peshawar — Russia Invades Persia — New Russo-
Persian Boundary—British Policy 116

CHAPTER VII.

THE FIRST AFGHAN WAR.

Lord Auckland's Policy in 1837—Case for Dost Muhammad stated by Sir John Kaye—Afghan Ideas of Hereditary Claims to Sovereignty—The Tripartite Treaty—The Army of the Indus—Passage through Sindh Delayed—Appointment of Macnaghten as Political Officer with the Expedition—English Gold Scattered Freely—Shah Suja's Reception at Candahar—Assault and Capture of Ghazni—Massacre of the Ghazis—Flight of Dost Muhammad beyond the Hindu Kush—Failure of Pursuit through Treachery of Haji Khan—Intrinsic Weakness of Shah Suja's Course Demonstrated—Cost of Living for English Officers at Cabul—Kaye's Judgment of the British "System" introduced into Afghanistan—Honours to the Victors—Designs of Further Interference Westwards—The Story of Colonel Stoddart and Arthur Conolly's "Missions"—Their Cruel Fate—Lord Ellenborough's Letter to the Amir of Bokhara—Brief Review of "The Afghan Tragedy" of 1838-42—Story of Dr. Brydon's Escape 137

CHAPTER VIII.

AFGHAN AFFAIRS AFTER THE WAR OF 1838—42.

The Real Cause of the Damage to England's Position in Central Asia from the Cabul Disaster—Lord Ellenborough's Policy in 1842—Native Views on the Evacuation of Afghanistan—Rawlinson's Opinion of the Afghans as Soldiers—England "The Burnt Child," and Afghanistan "The Fire"—Internal Affairs of Afghanistan between the Retreat of General Elphinstone and the Advance of General Pollock—Muhammad Shah Khan a Noble Exception to the Generality of the Afghans—Murder of Shah Suja, the Puppet-King—Accession of Fatih Jang—Akbar Khan Intrigues for Power

xvi   *Contents.*

PAGE
—Fall of Fatih Jang—Proclamation of Shuhpur—Lord Ellenborough's "Song of Triumph"—Policy with Regard to Dost Muhammad Khan—England's Afghan Policy from 1842 to 1852—Origin of the Persian War of 1856—Herat and Treaty of Paris of 1857—Virtual Disregard of Treaty by Persia—Dost Muhammad's Neutrality in 1856-58 Purchased—Policy of Subsidies Discussed—Cost of Afghan War—The Blood-feud between the Afghans and the English—Sir John Lawrence's Treaties with Dost Muhammad—Extent of Dost Muhammad's Dominions—He Subdues Candahar and Herat—His Death—Subsequent Anarchy in Afghanistan—Rival Claimants to the "Masnad"—Shere Ali, the Designated Successor—His Son, Yakub Khan, is made Governor of Herat—Afzul Khan Obtains Possession of Cabul, and is proclaimed Amir—Shere Ali's Defeat—Yakub Khan's Gallant Achievements—Shere Ali Restored in 1868—He Suspects Yakub Khan of Treachery—Yakub Demands to be acknowledged Heir-Apparent—Open Quarrel between the Amir and Yakub—Yakub's Flight — Reconciliation and Imprisonment — Other Claimants to the Succession 154

CHAPTER IX.

RUSSIAN ADVANCE EASTWARDS.

Chief Difficulty in understanding the Central Asian Question—Importance of the News of the Arrival of a Russian Mission at Cabul—Its Mention in Parliament—Treatment of the Russian Mission—Reason of Importance attached to Independence of Afghanistan—Excessive Cost of Present Indian Forces of Great Britain—Our Real Concern with Afghanistan—Two Schools of Opinion on our Indian Frontier Policy — Lord Beaconsfield's Definition of "The Afghan Question"—His Enunciation of England's Present Policy—Review of Negotiations with the Amir—Dost Muhammad's Virtue in abstaining from Revenge in 1857—Lord Lawrence's so-called "Masterly Inactivity"—Succeeded by Different Policy of "Mischievous Activity"—Recognition of Shere Ali—The Umballa Meeting between Lord Mayo and Shere Ali—Lord Mayo's Declaration to the Amir examined—Practical Assistance in Money and Arms to Shere Ali—Shere Ali's oversanguine Expectations—View taken of Lord Mayo's Proceedings by Home Government— Lord Mayo's Explanation — Correspondence concerning a "Neutral Zone"— How "Neutral

Zone" defined in 1872—Russian Expedition to Khiva—Its Importance to India—The Worth of Russian Assurances—Lord Granville's Remonstrances—Expedition against the Turkomans—Shere Ali's Alarm at Russia's Advance—Sends his Confidential Agent to Simla—His Proposals to Lord Northbrook—Failure of Negotiations—Shere Ali communicates with General Kaufmann — Further Russian Official Assurances — So-called Exploring Expedition in 1875—Expedition against Kizil Arvat in 1876—Russian Advance in Bokhara and Khokand—Choice of Three Routes for Russian Advance on Afghan Frontier—Projected Railways—Russian Activity in Central Asia in Spring of 1878—Last Reported Russian Assurance—Latest Advance towards India 178

CHAPTER X.

THE AFGHAN POLICY OF THE LAST TWO VICEROYS.

Résumé of Lord Northbrook's Negotiations with the Amir—Proposal to permit Sir D. Forsyth to return through Afghan Territory negatived—The "Grievances" of Shere Ali—Sir Lewis Pelly's Conference with the Afghan Agent in 1876—The Occupation of Quettah—Lord Lytton's Letters to Shere Ali—The English Envoy at Ali Musjid—Repulse of the Mission—False Account sent to England—Question of Peace or War reverts to Consideration of Necessity of "Rectification" of Frontier—Is Refusal to receive English Officers an Insult?—Rawlinson's Opinion of England's Policy in the Presence of Russian Agents at Cabul—Policy of English Cabinet in sending an *Ultimatum* to Shere Ali—Lord Northbrook on the Conduct of Russia and the Amir—And on Sir James Stephen's View of the Amir's "International" Rights 213

APPENDIX A.—New Route to India 235

APPENDIX B.—Russia and England in Asia 237

APPENDIX C.—Russia's Advance Compared with that of Alexander the Great 243

APPENDIX D.—Lord Lawrence on the Present Crisis 246

APPENDIX E.—Sale's Defence of Jalalabad. 253

INTRODUCTION.

A FEW weeks ago the writer of these lines looked down from a window near the site of old Temple Bar upon a scene of triumph. An English Premier was passing in his carriage of state through a double row of vociferating Londoners of the unmistakable Jingo type. His progress was now and again impeded by the enthusiasm of certain of the unwashed who insisted upon climbing upon the steps of their idol's chariot, and taking a close view of that idol's noble features. Over the remaining stone buttress of Temple Bar and its sham counterpart on the opposite side of the way two unicorns were conspicuous, and a banner bearing the now familiar device, "Peace with Honour." The *cortège* passed slowly on; the Sphinx-like occupant of the first coach bowing with undoubted satisfaction to the multitude. After the great man's carriage had disappeared, suddenly, almost as if by pre-arrangement, a fire-engine swept past at full speed, clearing the street, as if by magic, of its terror-stricken foot-passengers. One felt for a moment somewhat of wonder at the coincidence, and all sorts of absurd fancies crowded upon the mind. Of what was it the omen? Did the instant intelligence of a conflagration somewhere that was flashed upon the spectator by the appearance of the fire-engine, in immediate connection with the State-ceremony of a Prime Minister's triumphal procession, prefigure a concurrence of analogous events in the political world? All men know now how hollow was the "Peace," and how doubtful was the "Honour," that were said to have been secured at Berlin. The peace has barely survived the summer and autumn, and early winter sees us locked in a struggle, which at the best will severely tax our energies and strain our resources—for what? To satisfy that "Honour" which, we were told, had been amply vindicated at Berlin.

Those who least admire Lord Beaconsfield must be constrained, we think, to admit that he possesses, in a degree rarely excelled, the faculty of versatility, the crab-like power of grasping each new situation and adapting his own programme, itself by no means a fixed one at any time, to whatever novel circumstances present themselves, with such tact as to dazzle the multitude into the belief that he had all along foreseen, and with infinite sagacity had provided for them. The Secretary-of-State-for-India's despatch to the Viceroy, which saw the light in the

Times of 21st November, is the latest example of this feature in the Premier's character. No one supposes that the document in question was other than a manifesto for the benefit of the English public, intended to be a vindication of the policy of the present Government, which is quite willing to accept all the credit of what is likely to be approved, and to shift on to the shoulders of their predecessors of the opposite party the responsibility of all that is worthy of condemnation. Thus it is cleverly shown that the present difficulty is to be traced entirely to the follies of Lord Northbrook's Government, the blame of which is again ingeniously fathered upon Her Majesty's then Government at home (Mr. Gladstone's). If Lord Northbrook had only guaranteed the Amir's dominion against all his foreign enemies—just as Lord Beaconsfield has guaranteed Asiatic Turkey against Russia—all would have been well. The Amir would have accepted our handsome subsidies, and presents of arms, like a good boy, and been all the more prepared in consequence to give us battle whenever the blood-feud that has existed for the last forty years or more should break out again! Because Lord Northbrook, or rather Mr. Gladstone, declined to pledge England to support Shere Ali in every case against foreign foes—a pledge which, if once given, would have encouraged that ruler in all sorts of aggression upon

xxii   *Introduction.*

his neighbours—the Amir became sullen and reserved. From 1874 to the present time it has been the constant endeavour of the Premier and his colleagues to break down this reserve and remove this sullenness. The promise of protection and active countenance which Shere Ali had vainly desired from Lord Northbrook has been offered to him—coupled with the condition that English Agents should be given access to positions in his territories other than at Cabul itself. The offer was refused, and has been continually refused ever since.

It is quietly assumed that it would have been accepted if made by Lord Northbrook. We question very much if it would have met with any other response then than the one given now. Shere Ali was willing to accept our guarantee, our subsidies, and our guns, but whether he would ever have consented to admit British Agents, and so become reduced—in his own eyes, at least—to much the same position as that held by such semi-independent Indian potentates as Scindia, the Nizam, and Nepal, is more than doubtful. This argument, however, suits Lord Beaconsfield's purpose admirably, which is to show that the present war has been really necessitated by the perverse conduct of Mr. Gladstone's Government.

In effect it does not seem that the apportionment of praise and blame is to be made so easily. The wisdom that comes after events will always be able to indicate where a fault has been committed which it can be shown has entailed disaster that might otherwise have been averted. If we were to venture to indicate the weak point in the recent foreign policy of England, we should find it in the exaggerated idea of Russia's designs upon India which some Englishmen entertain. That Power seems rather to require peace to recover herself after the recent devastating war with Turkey than a war which shall urge her still further to the verge of bankruptcy. It is premature now to discuss the morality of the present invasion of Afghanistan. It *may* be justifiable, and we must hope for the honour of England that ample reason will be forthcoming to satisfy both the English Parliament and the English people that we have not violated right in order to obtain for ourselves a doubtful advantage.

Messina, November 28, 1878.

AFGHANISTAN

AND

THE CENTRAL ASIAN QUESTION.

CHAPTER I.

AFGHANISTAN—ITS NATURAL FEATURES.

Natural Boundaries—Approximate Extent of Afghanistan—Origin of Name—Independent Territory—What Afghan Dominions Include—Comparison of Afghanistan with Switzerland—Mountain-ranges—Hindu Kush and its Prolongations—Safed Koh—Suliman Mountains—Passes on the Indo-Afghan Frontier—Fort of Ali Musjid—Natural Divisions—Rivers—Lakes—Provinces and Towns.

AFGHANISTAN, or, as its name signifies, the land of the Afghans, may be roughly compared in area with Germany. The north-eastern part, called the Cabul valley, from the river of that name which waters it, is really the upper dominating section of the Indus basin; and there is some ground, therefore, for the statement which has been made that physically, at least, Eastern Afghanistan is part and parcel of India. And if all the nationalities of the earth were to strike for "natural boundaries," India might have as good a right to claim the Cabul valley as her own as Spain would have to include Portugal, or Germany to take Belgium and Holland.

What was said just now as to the extent of Afghanistan must be regarded as a mere approximation to the truth, for the best maps can only keep pace with skilled explorers, and these have been few and far between in the countries between the Oxus and the Indus, so that accurate information is not yet to be had on many interesting points connected with their natural features. Enough, however, can be gathered for a rough conception of them from scattered notes of hasty travellers, who passed through the country keeping, so to speak, one eye on the scenery and the other on their holsters. The name, it should be premised, by which the country is known so extensively outside its own limits, is only as old as the short-lived Durani empire of Ahmed Shah in the middle of the last century. The Afghans rarely use the term, speaking of themselves as Pushtanu (plural of Pushtú), and their country as Wiláyat. The whole Afghan dominions, including, in addition to Afghanistan Proper,* that part of the Oxus basin to which the name Afghan

* Afghanistan Proper is nearly co-extensive with the ancient provinces of *Aria* (Herat), *Drangiana* (Seistan), the region of the *Paropamisadæ* (Cabul), and *Arachosia* (Candahar), with *Gandaritis* (Peshawar and the lands of the Yuzufzais). Of the latter district part now is the British district of Peshawar, and the rest independent.

Its Natural Features.

Turkestan has been applied, may be regarded as a quadrilateral plateau, about 600 miles from east to west, and 600 miles from north to south. Excluding Afghan Turkestan, the extent of the country from north to south must be decreased to 450 miles. Both in the larger and smaller areas there would be included some territory which is free from Afghan control altogether, and other tracts over which the hold of the Amir is spasmodic and precarious.

Examples of the former are the valleys north of Peshawar in the possession of the Yuzufzais; those to the west and south-west of the same district, occupied by the Mohmands, Afridis, Vaziris, and other tribes; and the elevated valleys of Chitral or Kashgar, and of the independent Kafirs (non-Muhammadans) among the higher spurs of the Hindu Kush. To the semi-independent territories belong the eastern districts of Khost and of Kuram, which are conterminous with British territory; the Kakar country in the extreme south-west; and part of the mountain region in the north-west, inhabited by the Eimaks and Hazaras; to which may probably be added Badakhshan.

The boundaries of Afghanistan, roughly stated, and subject to correction on account of some independent and semi-independent territories included by them, may be thus defined :—

The Oxus forms the northern boundary line from

its source in Pamir to Khoja Salih Ferry in 65° E. long. nearly. Thence the Afghan territories become conterminous with those of Khiva, the line that divides them running south-west, and skirting the Turkoman desert to the Murghab river, and passing thence in the same direction to a point on the Hari Rud river, a few miles south of Sarakhs, in about lat. 36°.

On the west, the boundary line runs from the last-mentioned point, first south-east for a short distance, and then nearly due south to about 30° N. lat., where it bends eastward across Lake Hamun or Seistan, and again turns westward, being continued to the intersection of lat. 30° with the lake, including, from its point of divergence to its termination, a triangular tract which forms part of the plain of Seistan. All to the west of this line is Persia.

On the south there is no natural boundary, and it can only be roughly given as a line from the Lake of Seistan, in lat. 30° to the Helmand river, and thence south-east to Nushki, whence it runs north-east through the southern valleys of the Lova, dividing the Pishin valley from Quettah, or the Shal territory, belonging to the Baluch state of Kelat. Further east, the boundary line has a southern declination, and terminates not far from the Indus.

The eastern boundary from a point a few miles distant from Mittan Kot, on the Indus, is formed by the eastern spurs of the Suliman Mountains as far as Peshawar, and thence northward the boundary is for a time the Indus, but thereafter lies in almost unknown country.

Except portions of the lower valley of the Cabul river, small tracts towards the Indus, and the space included in a triangle formed by joining Herat, Candahar, and the extreme south-west point of the Lake of Seistan, the whole of the quadrilateral plateau of Afghanistan has a minimum height of 4,000 feet above the sea. A tract that would be indicated by a straight line of 200 miles drawn from the Kushan Pass in the Hindu Kush Mountains, passing about 35 miles west of Cabul to Rangak, on the road between Ghazni and Candahar, is nowhere less than 7,000 feet above the sea. The lowest level taken—that of a position in the Lake of Seistan—is 1,280 feet above the sea. Herat is 2,650, Candahar 3,490.

Briefly, then, Afghanistan Proper is an elevated table land, having an area of more than 211,500 square miles, somewhat larger than France, and is bounded, on the north by Turkestan and Khiva, on the west by Persia, on the south by Baluchistan, and on the east by the Panjab. Westward of the Hindu Kush the Koh-i-Baba cuts off Afghanistan Proper from the tract known as Afghan Turkestan, which reaches down to the bank of the Oxus, and includes the various minor Khanates or States of Kunduz, Khulum, Balkh with Akcha, and the *Chahar Wilayat*, or "Four Domains" of Sir-i-pul, Shibrghan, Andkhui, and Maimana, together with such of the Hazara tribes as lie north of the Hindu Kush and its prolongation in the Koh-i-Baba. Besides these the name Afghanistan is sometimes made to include also Badakhshan, a poor mountain tract between the Hindu Kush and the Oxus, which, though nominally it forms part of the Amir's dominions, is of small value to its suzerain, the tribute annually paid to Cabul being said to amount to no more than about £1,500. The barren mountains which compose Badakhshan can hardly, indeed, be said to belong to Afghanistan by other than a precarious tenure of suzerainty or protection, since the present princes obtained the territory by the aid of Shere Ali, from their uncle, who was anxious to become the feudatory of the Bokharan ruler.

It has been pointed out that the main features of the coast-line of Europe are repeated on a grander scale in Asia. The peninsula of Spain and Portugal finds its counterpart in Arabia; France in Asia Minor and Persia; Italy in India; Turkey, Greece, and the Grecian Archipelago, in Burmah, Siam, and the Eastern Archipelago; and Russia in the Chinese Empire; while the British Isles on the west of the Euro-Asian Continent are placed symmetrically with Japan on the east. So striking

Its Natural Features. 7

has the parallelism between Italy and India seemed to some writers, that they have not hesitated to state that the Himalayas are repeated in the Alps; the Rhone and the Po in the Indus and Ganges; while Genoa (or Marseilles) is Karachi; Venice, Calcutta; Milan, Delhi; Naples, Bombay; and Sicily, Ceylon.

If the authors of this comparison had carried it a little further inland, they would hardly have failed to find a counterpart of Switzerland in Afghanistan. Whether or not an ingenious geographer could find the representatives of all the chief natural features, such as mountains, plains, rivers, and lakes, in sufficient correspondence to bear out the comparison, it cannot but be evident that in its relations to India on the east, Persia on the west, and Asiatic Russia on the north, Afghanistan is physically situated with regard to them, not dissimilarly from the position that Switzerland holds with reference to Italy and Austria on the east, France on the west, and Germany on the north. Baluchistan, however, which is the southern boundary of the Amir's dominions, is not yet so completely British-Indian as Piedmont and Lombardy are Italian.

To give a detailed account of the mountain system of Afghanistan would be to transcend the modest limits of this work. A rough outline may, however, be attempted. It has been a common error with some journalists of late years to describe

Afghanistan as lying beyond the Himalayas. It really lies within the Hindu Kush section of that Indian mountain girdle. Or, to be still more correct, the Western Himalayas are extended into Afghanistan, and form four mountain regions, which are known from east to west by the names Hindu Kush, Paghman Mountains, Koh-i-Baba, and Ghor Mountains. The last were known to the Greeks as the Paropamisus, and consist of two parallel chains, collectively called by Persian historians the Ghor Mountains, but distinguished now, the northern as the Safed Koh, or White Mountains, and the southern as the Siyah Koh, or Black Mountains.

To take all the northern mountains in order, we find between 34° and 35° N. lat. two very lofty mountain-ranges, between which flows the Indus. To both of these the name of Himalaya Mountains is applied as far as long. 70°, the eastern being undoubtedly a part of the great Indian northern mountain barrier, and the western as certainly a continuation of it. A glance at the map will, however, show that this western range, although it rises in some places as high as 20,000 feet, and runs from east-south-east to west-north-west, does not form the watershed of the rivers of this region. For the watershed, according to most geographers, we must look farther north to a range called the Karakoram Mountains, which run almost due east and west, and are clearly a continuation of the Kuenlun Mountains, which stretch across Tibet into China. This western continuation of the Kuenlun is called in Afghanistan the Hindu Kush, or Hindu Koh (" koh," in Persian, meaning mountain). It will be observed, further, that the Indian range of the Himalayas and the Hindu Kush do not run parallel, but converge and unite in one mountain-mass between 70° and 69° east longitude, including between them the country known to the Afghans as Kafiristan (the land of the infidels, *i.e.*, non-Muhammadans).

Thus it seems to be optional with us to regard the Hindu Kush as an extension of either the Karakoram or the Himalaya range of mountains, or, better still, as the continuation in a single chain of both.

Only the northern declivity of the Western Himalayas is included in Kafiristan, the southern belonging to Afghanistan. From the plains these mountains appear to rise in terraces, so that as many as four ridges, one overtopping the other, may at some places be seen. There are wide valleys among them, but only a narrow strip of cultivable soil along the line of drainage. Between the higher portion of the ridges, and the base of the hills, is an inclined plane—often very wide—strewed or entirely covered with boulders and shingle, without a particle of soil. On the declivity of the hills, however, where the inclination of the upper strata is less perpendicular, there is found a rich soil of some depth. Advantage is taken of this for cultivation, and, where this has not been done, high forest trees occupy the ground to an elevation of 10,000 feet above the sealevel. Up to 4,500 feet these consist chiefly of a species of oak, called "balut"; but beyond that height they are largely mixed with a kind of olive, called "zaitun," up to 6,500 feet, where it gives place to the "deodara." These forests are the most extensive in Afghanistan.

From the point of convergence of the Himalayas with the Hindu Kush, at about 70° E. long., the sides of the mountains are destitute of trees, and are devoid of soil, the rocks protruding in every direction, and huge angular *débris* occupying the intervening spaces. Dry and thorny bushes are the only vegetation, as far as 68° E. long., where the Hindu Kush, strictly so-called, comes to an end in a huge snowclad mountain-mass, called by that name, which rises to the height of 15,000 feet above the level of the sea.

The best-known of the many populous valleys in this region is the Panjshir valley, which has a total length of seventy miles, and an average width of about a mile and a-half. There are some seven thousand families living in the lower part, the upper being uninhabited, on account of the extreme cold in winter. Although the soil is naturally very poor, it is extensively cultivated, orchards and mulberry groves constituting most of the wealth of the people in these valleys; the mulberries, when dried, yielding a flour which is their principal food. Through this valley passes the high road from Cabul to Kunduz, and at its upper end it traverses the famous Khawak Pass, at a height of 13,200 feet above the sea. Through another similar valley, further to the west, watered by the Parwan river, passes another road across the Hindu Kush (by the Sar-alang Pass), leading to the plain of the Oxus.

After running south-west, as just described, for some 370 miles, the Hindu Kush ceases to be locally known by that name, although it is still applied to the whole chain of northern mountains. This chain is continued in the smaller range of the Paghman Mountains, which run nearly due south, and are of lower elevation. This range consists of two parallel ridges, with a valley between them of nearly ten miles in width, having an elevation that seldom sinks below 10,000 feet above the sea, and is, consequently, unfitted for cultivation. It affords, however, a grateful refuge from the summer heats to the pastoral tribes in its neighbourhood. The two enclosing ridges are from 12,000 to 13,000 feet high, and, being free from snow in the summer, several passes lead over them to the valley of Bamian, which lies west of the western range, and is only 8,500 feet above the sea. Of these passes the best known are the Irak, attaining nearly 13,000 feet; the Kallu, 12,480 feet; and the Hajiyak, 12,190 feet above the sea.

Where the Paghman Mountains end, the Koh-i-Baba rises as a single range, and runs due west. Of these mountains we have very much yet to learn. We know that they commence at their eastern extremity in an immense mass of rocks about 14,000 feet high, with still loftier snow-clad peaks above them that attain 15,000 feet at least. To the westward the range is continued in a series of lofty peaks, and then breaks up into three parallel ranges, enclosing the waters of the Murghab and Hari-rud rivers. The northernmost of these finally loses itself in the sands of the Turkoman desert; the middle one, the Koh-i-Safed, or White Mountains, has a westerly and longer course, running north of and past Herat, where it turns northward and also merges into the desert; while the southern range, called Koh-i-Siyah, or Black Mountains, follows a course pretty nearly parallel with the last-named one, and, it is believed, eventually unites with the ranges that form the northern boundary of Persia as far as the Caspian. If this theory be proved to be a physical fact, there would be shown to exist an unbroken connection between the mountain systems of the Caucasus and the Eastern Himalayas. Indeed, the whole line of Alpine watershed which we have been describing, stretching from the southern end of Pamir across Afghanistan to Mash-had in Khorasan was known to Alexander's historian as the Caucasus —a fact which seems to indicate that the probable continuity of the ranges was even then surmised. The southern spurs of the Koh-i-Siyah give rise to the Khash-rud and Harut-rud rivers and to some feeders of the Helmand river.

A recent writer in the *Geographical Magazine* gives a somewhat different statement of the connection of the Hindu Kush proper with its western extensions. He regards the Koh-i-Baba as the direct continuation westward of the Hindu Kush from the point where it changes its direction from the south-west. A saddle connects the Hindu Kush here with the Paghman range, which encloses the head streams of the Helmand and Ghorband rivers, and runs south-west, forming the water-parting between the Helmand and Argandab, and ceasing at their confluence. According to this account the two Paghman ridges are offshoots from the Hindu Kush, and not links in the chain.

A spur from the Paghman range runs westward, enclosing the source of the Argandab, and thence extending parallel with the northern chain, bounding throughout its length the table-land of Ghazni and the home of the Ghilzais, and ceasing just north of Candahar.

Along the parallel of 34° runs, due east and west, the Safed-Koh range (not to be confounded with the western range of that name which forms part of the Paropamisan or Ghor Mountains), which constitutes the southern water-shed of the Cabul basin. It consists of a single range for about seventy-five miles, when it splits into two ridges. Its connection with the Hindu Kush by means of the Attakoh range has been asserted. The main range of the Safed-Koh, which preserves a pretty uniform level of about 12,500 feet in height, is richly clad with pine, almond, and other trees. Its valleys abound in orchards, cultivated fields and gardens, and mulberry, pomegranate, and other fruit trees are plentiful. It is considered by some geographers that a network of low mountains runs generally south from this range, and is merged in the table-land of Kelat and the mountainous system of Baluchistan.

Next in importance to this great northern range of the Hindu Kush is the eastern range, known as the Suliman Mountains, which on the map appear to form the natural frontier line between the Afghan table-land and the plains of the Indus. This is the name applied by the best authorities to the range, or ranges, running almost due north and south along the meridian of 70° E. ; from the Gomal Pass to the twenty-ninth parallel of latitude, or thereabouts. Major Raverty has described it as a mighty mountain barrier, containing in its northern section two ranges which increase in number as they run southwards, till at its southern extremity, where the Sari river breaks through, there are as many as twelve distinct ridges, " like battalions in columns of companies at quarter distance." The mountains increase in height from east to west, and the highest, called Mihtar-Suliman, or Koh-i-Sujah, is snow-capped in winter.

Colonel Macgregor holds a different view respecting this range. As one running north and south along the meridian of 70°, he does not recognise the Suliman at all. He considers that from the Attakoh range, between Cabul and Ghazni, there springs a range of mountains which proceeds southward without a break, throwing out spurs to the east and west, and that this is the range which forms the system of mountains of Eastern Afghanistan and Baluchistan. The weight of authority, however, is opposed to this view.

A peculiarity in connection with this range—the Suliman—is noticeable in the large number of streams that pierce through its sides after draining the table-lands to the west. These naturally afford access, by means of the passes they form, from the valley of the Indus to the high plateaus of Afghanistan.

PASSES ON THE INDO-AFGHAN FRONTIER.

This seems to be the proper place to speak of these gaps in the great mountain barrier that stretches from the Oxus to the Indian Ocean, by which commerce penetrates from Central Asia to India, and which formerly afforded paths to the invading hosts that poured down to obtain the plunder of her rich cities. The four best-known passes on the eastern frontier of Afghanistan are the Khaibar, Kuram, Gomal, and Bolan. Besides these there are innumerable others of every degree of practicability, most of which are known only by native report. In speaking of these passes, it must be remembered that the names thus broadly given, locally apply to only a particular part of the whole distance to be traversed before reaching the tableland beyond. Thus, what is commonly called the Khaibar Pass includes a succession of gorges or defiles, each designated by its own special name. The Khaibar Pass may be said, generally speaking, to commence at Jamrud, ten miles west of Peshawar, and to extend to Dhaka, a distance of about thirty-three miles. The actual entrance to the defile, however, is at Kadam, a place three miles out of Jamrud, which is a small village surrounded by a mud wall.

This is (or was) the site of an old Sikh fort, which was built in 1837, after the Afghan army, under the famous sons of Dost Muhammad, Akbar Khan and Afzal Khan, had taken to flight at the unexpected arrival of Ranjit Sinh, whose famous march with a relieving army from Guzerat has been seldom equalled. Within 1,000 yards of Kadam the gorge narrows to 150 yards, with steep, precipitous cliffs on either hand. Between this and the Afghan frontier fort of Ali Musjid, distant about ten miles, the mountains on either hand are about 1,500 feet in height, slaty, bare, and, to all appearance, inaccessible. The width of the Pass varies in this part from 290 to 40 feet. The name of this fort figured for a few days early in October last, rather conspicuously in the Indian telegrams published in the London daily papers. It was incorrectly stated that our troops had marched upon it from Jamrud, and captured it from the Afghans. It was just below Ali Musjid, too, that Major Cavagnari was in September 21st, 1878, told by the Afghan officer, the Mir Akhor or Master of the Horse, that the British Mission would not be allowed to proceed on its projected journey to Cabul.

It was here that the colloquy occurred at which, it was alleged, language of menace was used by the Afghan officer, the report of which, filtering through the inflamed channels of fiery special correspondents, roused a section of the English people to a sense of gross insult received, and for a time induced some of the strongest opponents of Lord Beaconsfield's Government to clamour for immediate redress. Of the exact nature of these proceedings between the Afghan and English officers we shall come to speak later on. We may mention here that the little fort of Ali Musjid takes its name from the ruins of a small Muhammadan mosque ("Musjid" being Persian for mosque) in its vicinity. Its situation is nearly midway between Peshawar and Dhaka, about ten miles from the eastern end of the Khaibar Pass, as above stated, and twenty-six miles from the western end, while it is seventy miles from Jalalabad. It stands on the south side of the Pass, at the height of 2,433 feet above the sea, on the summit of beetling crags, which tower perpendicularly above the roadway. The crests of the hills at this spot are barely 150 yards from each other; and as on the northern slopes a smaller masonry blockhouse has been constructed, a very effective cross-fire can be poured on troops advancing through the defile. The fort itself is said to be not more than 150 feet long and 60 feet wide, and is commanded, fortunately for an invader from the Indian side, by higher positions, both on the south and west. It was by attacking it on these faces that Colonel Wade succeeded in taking it in 1839. Although, however, he commenced the attack on the 25th of July, and was enabled in a few hours to drive the defenders from their outworks by the accuracy of his shell-fire, the Afghans being armed only with matchlocks, it was not until three days later that the place surrendered. Its garrison was under 1,000 strong, of whom 500 were irregular Jazailchis (matchlock men), the remainder being levies from the Afridi and Shinwari tribes. Wade's loss was over 150 killed and wounded. After its capture the fort was placed under a garrison of Yusufzai Pathans, with the object of keeping open free communication between Peshawar and our forces in Jalalabad and Cabul. In November, 1841, a desperate attack was made on the fort by a body of about 2,000 men belonging to the neighbouring Afghan tribes. They cut off the water supply, and reduced the place to dreadful straits; but the British commandant, Lieutenant Mackeson, with his usual fertility of resource, bought them off. A force, under Colonel Moseley, consisting of 2,500, was then sent to hold it; but, owing to insufficiency of provisions, that officer was compelled to retire in eight days, with the loss of 180 killed and wounded. Sir George Pollock, on his advance through the Khaibar with the avenging army in 1842, left a garrison in Ali Musjid; and on evacuating Afghanistan in November of the same year, he destroyed the works, but they were speedily reconstructed by the orders of Dost Muhammad.

The great drawback to the occupation of this advanced fort is its extreme unhealthiness. In 1839 the mortality in the British detachment holding it under Colonel Wade was something terrible. In less than eight weeks there were 250 deaths out of a strength of a little over 2,400 men. This was mainly owing to the water, which is strongly impregnated with antimony; and even this supply is only obtained from the Khaibar stream below, so that the place can easily be forced into capitulation, should time be no object with an advancing army. It would have been unwise in the present instance to have exposed our troops to the sickness that proved so fatal forty years ago, unless an immediate advance upon Cabul had been intended. Several roads, moreover, are known to us now by which this position of Ali Musjid, the most formidable obstacle between Peshawar and Jalalabad, can be completely turned, so that its capture under the circumstances was wisely deferred. Among these roads are the Tatara road, which enters the hills about nine miles north of Jamrud, and joins the main route at Dhaka. The Kadapa road, and one through the Bara Valley also—both of them avoid Ali Musjid—are practicable for lightly-equipped columns.

After this digression, which the importance that has been attached in some quarters to the early capture of the fort of Ali Musjid seemed to warrant, we continue the description of the Khaibar Pass. For a distance of two and a-half miles beyond Ali Musjid it retains its difficult character. It then enters the Lala Beg Valley, about six miles in length, with an average breadth of a mile and a-half. The western end of the valley finds the road entering a still narrower defile, there being scarcely room in it for two camels to pass each other. The Landi Khana Pass—which is by some said to be the highest point in the Khaibar—is distant from this point about a mile and a-half, the ascent over it being narrow, rugged, steep, and generally the most difficult part of the road. Guns could not be drawn here except by men, and then only after the improvement of the track. The descent, however, is along a well-made road, and is not so difficult. On the west side of the Pass the mountains gradually open out, and lose much of their inaccessible nature. Dhaka is distant about eight miles, and here the defile ends. The main road to Cabul is continued from this point through other passes to the town and fortress of Jalalabad—famous for General Sale's defence of it in 1842—passing on the way through the villages of Lalpura, Hazarnau, Basawal, Batikot, Chardeh, Bari Kab, and Ali Baghan. From Peshawar to Jalalabad by road is about ninety miles, and thence to Cabul, through the Jagdallak, Lattaband, Khurd Cabul, and other passes, is 100 miles. It was in these latter defiles, within a few marches of Cabul, that the "Cabul massacre" occurred, and not in the Khaibar Pass, which none of the unfortunate army ever reached on that occasion.

Of the passes to the north of the Khaibar the most important are the Baroghil and Karambar passes leading from Cashmere, our outlying feudatory principality, to Khokand, the latest officially announced Russian acquisition in Central Asia. They also lead from Kashgar to Cabul and Cashmere by routes that cross at Chitral. The Baroghil Pass is known to us from the reports of the Mullah employed by Colonel Montgomerie, who travelled from Chitral into Badakhshan by this route.

Captain Biddulph, who was attached to Sir Douglas Forsyth's mission, visited Sarhad, the town at the northern extremity of the Pass, but it is doubtful if any Englishman has traversed these routes throughout. Khokand, or Farghana, is separated from British territory by the Pamir Plateau, and although the actual distance in a direct line between the Czar's territory and ours is not much greater than 200 miles at this point, yet the road that connects them is not one which a modern army could follow. Leaving Khokand (1,540 feet above the sea), it passes through

Marghilan to Uch Kurgan (3,100 feet). These places are said to have been the scenes of indiscriminate slaughter of the Khokandians in the campaign of January, 1876. Bearing south, the road passes through Isfairam, and over the Little Alai Plateau, which stands 12,000 feet above sea level; then, crossing the Great Alai, at an altitude of 14,000 feet, it descends into the valley of Muk Su, following a south-easterly course to Sirich; bending round to the west it strikes the Oxus at Kila Panjab, the elevation of which is 9,090 feet; then, ascending the stream to Sarhad, which Biddulph determined to be 10,975 feet, the road crosses the Baroghil fifteen miles to the southward, the altitude being 12,000 feet. From this point a road branches off to Mastoj, and, following the course of the Kunad stream, passes through Chitral (7,140 feet), Dir, and Pashat to Jalalabad.

At Chitral another road from Samarcand, through Penjakand, Hissar, Kolab, Faizabad, and Zebak, joins this route. The road through the Baroghil Pass into Cashmere is a most difficult and mountainous pathway. It touches few villages, the chief being Yasin, in Afghan territory (height 7,770 feet), and crosses the Maharajah of Cashmere's border at Gaon Kuch. It then runs through Gilgit (5,270 feet) to Bunji on the Indus, and so through Iskardo and Dras to Sirinagar.

The Karambar Pass is merely a subsidiary road to that by the Baroghil. Leaving Sarhad, it follows a more easterly course, passing by the Karambar Lake and joining the main road at Gaon Kuch on the frontier.

These passes, it seems, were recently secured for us by the Maharajah of Cashmere's troops, but the danger to be apprehended from that side is not very great, owing to the enormous natural difficulties of the road.

Along the north-western frontier there are innumerable passes, of which at least seventeen are well-defined roads, practicable for the movements of lightly-equipped columns, and there are certainly four up which guns could be taken. Of these, the Khaibar, already described, and the Bolan are the best known, the Kuram and Gomal being the other two chief ones. The great drawback to the two latter being utilised in the event of war is the fact that our means of communication within our own border are of a very imperfect kind, so that some military authorities are of opinion that the difficulties a force would encounter before it could reach the eastern end of the Kuram or Gomal Passes, would be almost as great as those to be met with in the mountains themselves.

The Kuram Pass is so called from the river of that name, which debouches through it and flows south-west through Thal and Bannu to the Indus, receiving as tributaries the Shamil, Tochi, Gambela, and other streams. The road through the Kuram Valley, which was traversed by Sir H. Lumsden's Mission in 1857, leads from Thal to Ghazni and Cabul, the route to the latter city branching off near the Shutargardan (Camel's Neck) Pass, north-west of the Paiwar. By this route, Cabul is distant from Thal not more than 150 miles. There is a longer road, available at seasons when the Shutargardan is not so, which follows the Ghazni road as far as Khushi. It is described as a fairly good road, but the turbulent conduct of the Jajis involved Lumsden's party in great difficulties. These tribes being hardly restrained by the Amir's troops from massacring the mission—a fact which will scarcely warrant our regarding them as very friendly to us. The climate of the Kuram Valley is described as being magnificent: for about six weeks the winter is severe, but during the spring and autumn it is most charming. It is very fertile, filled with orchards, and exceedingly well cultivated.

The Gomal Pass is the next in importance, and is similarly formed by a river, from which it is named. General Chamberlain in 1860 led a force against the Mahsuds up the Zam Valley from Tank, to the north of the Gomal River. Kaniguram, the capital, was taken, and considerable chastisement inflicted on the marauding tribe. From the facts collected during this expedition is derived most of our knowledge of the Gomal Pass, which leads direct to Ghazni, and is credited with being the route by which Mahmud of Ghazni made most of his invasions of India.

Besides the Drapan Pass, from Dera Ismail Khan, and others north and south of it, Major Raverty gives details of no less than thirty-four passes (exclusive of small ones) between the Kaura and the Sari. These are too distant from the Indus to be of much use for military purposes. The principal are the Kaura, Vihowa, Barkoi, Wrug, Trundi, Saunra, Sari, and Vador Passes, the last of which leads from Dera Ghazi Khan.

The Bolan Pass leads direct to Quettah, which is at present our most advanced post westward, being beyond the 67th degree of longitude, while Cabul itself is to the east of the 69th degree. Sir John Kaye speaks of the Bolan as commencing at Dadur, but it is, perhaps, more correct to say that it begins about five miles to the north-west of that place. From Shikarpur in Sindh to Dadur is 146 miles, and this distance was traversed by the Bengal column in February and March, 1839, in sixteen painful marches. Water and forage were so scarce that the cattle suffered terribly on the way, the camels falling dead by scores on the desert. The Bolan Pass is 60 miles in length, and the passage was accomplished by the column just spoken of in six days. It is everywhere practicable for artillery, and, though formidable in appearance—in one part being only from 70 feet to 80 feet broad, with steep cliffs on each side—can be easily forced by a British column. Its summit is stated to be 5,800 feet above sea-level, and its average ascent 90 feet to the mile. At Sir-i-Bolan (the head of the Pass) a mountain-torrent sometimes bars the way during the height of the rainy season. On emerging from the Bolan Pass the traveller enters the beautiful valley of Shal, "a favoured spot in a country of little favour." The clear, crisp climate is one peculiarly suited to the European constitution, and over the wide plain, bounded by noble mountain-ranges, intersected by many sparkling streams, and dotted with orchards and vineyards, the eye ranges with delight. Quettah itself, which is ten miles off, is described by Hough as "a most miserable mud town, with a small castle on a mound, on which there was a small gun on a rickety carriage."

There are other passes besides the Bolan through the Brahu range, of which the principal are the Mula, Nagau, and Bhor Passes. The Mula, otherwise known as the Gandava, follows the windings of the Mula river, which has to be crossed repeatedly, and is considerably to the south of the Bolan. It leads through Nard to Kelat, a cross-road leading through Gaz to Khozdar, a Baluch town of some importance.

Anjira, a village at the top of the Pass, is at an elevation of 5,250 feet, but the inclination is, on an average, only 45 feet to the mile for the whole distance—102 miles. This greater length, and the fact that it only leads to Kelat—which is 100 miles south of Quettah—render the Bolan, although a more difficult road, the preferable one for an advance upon Candahar.

NATURAL DIVISIONS OF AFGHANISTAN.

Having taken a rapid survey of the mountain systems of Afghanistan, and the means by which access is to be had to her chief cities from the one side of Russian Turkestan and British India, we pass on to consider the natural divisions of the country. These we shall find it convenient to classify as follows:—

(I.) The Valley or Basin of the Cabul River.

(II.) The Central Table-land, on which stand Ghazni and Kalât-i-Ghilzai, embracing the upper valleys of ancient *Arachosia*.

(III.) The Upper Helmand Basin.

(IV.) The Lower Helmand Basin, embracing Giriskh, and the Afghan portion of Seistan.

(V.) The Basin of the Herat River; and

(VI.) The Eastern Portion of the Table-land, draining by streams, which are chiefly occasional torrents, towards the Indus.

To these some add—

(VII.) The northern mountain regions ; and,

(VIII.) The Southern Table-land, lying between the Khoja Amram range and the Muri and Bugti mountains, and descending to the west, where it terminates in the desert of Baluchistan, just short of 65° E. long.

(I.) *The Valley of the Cabul River.*—This has its northern limit in the range of the Hindu Kush, beginning on the west at the foot of the Paghman Mountains, and stretching eastward to the banks of the Indus, a distance of about 200 miles, in a straight line. In the extreme west the valley is 10,000 feet above the sea ; but at its eastern end, near the Indus, it is not more than 750 feet above sea level. The southern boundary of the valley is formed by an uninterrupted chain of heights of varying deviation, which is separated from the Paghman range by the narrow plain, called the Valley of Maidan, which is 7,747 feet above the sea and is well cultivated.

The road from Cabul to Ghazni and Candahar passes through this plain. To the east of this road commences the chain just spoken of, which consists at first of isolated hills of moderate elevation. They are described as low, with little grass, bad water, and treeless, their dismal appearance corresponding with that of other mountain regions that have been found to contain great metallic riches. While the English occupation existed many beds of very rich copper ore were discovered in several places, but the natives work them only to a small extent.

At Tazin, twenty miles from Maidan, these hills change their aspect, rising higher and becoming clothed with trees. They merge into the Safedkoh range, of which, indeed, they may be considered the western extension, this elevated rocky mass occupying a distance of some thirty to forty miles from west to east, and from fifteen to twenty miles from north to south.

The highest summits of the Safed Koh reach to 16,000 feet above the sea, and the sides are covered to the height of 10,000 feet, with forests, chiefly of deodara, while orchards, cultivated fields, and pasture-grounds skirt the base. The peaks are snow-capped all the year round, and from the snow rise many streams, that flow uninterruptedly through the summer.

The high mountains of the Safed Koh terminate at about 70° E. long., and the Tira or Khaibar hills, that succeed them to the east, are of lower elevation, declining steadily in height as they approach the Indus.

The northern slopes of the Khaibar hills are steep, and generally bare, or clothed with scanty

Its Natural Features. 31

grass, except after the autumnal rains. There are plateaus of some extent, however, on these high hills, which have a deep soil, and furnish good crops where irrigation is possible.

The Cabul river (the *Cophen* of Alexander) rises in the Unai Pass, about thirty-seven miles west of Cabul, in the near neighbourhood of the source of its rival, the Helmand. It drains the Maidan valley, and below Cabul is joined by the Logar river, which flows north from the Ghilzai plateau.

It flows in a westerly course for about 300 miles, draining the southern slopes of the Hindu Kush on the left and the northern watershed of the Safed Koh on the right, and falls into the Indus at Attok. Its tributaries on the right are numerous, but, excepting the Logar, are insignificant in volume, owing to the nearness of the watershed. On the north or left bank the Cabul river receives the large streams of the Panjshir, Alishang, Kunar, and Landai Sin. Of these the Kunar or Chitral river is the longest, and, indeed, as regards length, might count as the main stream. Higher up in its course it is called the *river of Kashgar* and the *Bailam*, and has been identified with the *Choaspes* and *Malaniantus* of the ancients. It rises in a small lake near the borders of Pamir, and flows in a south-west direction through the length of Kashgar, its whole length to its junction with the Cabul river being not less than 250 miles. The Cabul river, in part of its course, between Cabul and Jalalabad, descends 4,000 feet in fifty miles, and its banks and bed consist of huge rocks. The lowest ford (a dry season one) is near Jalalabad, before the junction of the river with the Kunar. From this point a safe and rapid descent is made by means of rafts on inflated skins, and boats of 50 tons can be floated from Jalalabad downwards. During the floods the distance between Jalalabad and Peshawar (not less than 100 miles) can be traversed in this way in twelve hours. The river is lowest in the winter, and is at its greatest height in August, when the upper snows begin to descend.

At a point sixty miles from the Kunar confluence, the Cabul river issues from the mountains, by which it has been hitherto hemmed in, and enters the plain of Peshawar. It soon after receives the Landai Sin, which is the name given to the joint streams of the Swat and Panj Kora, which drain the great valleys of the Yuzufzais; *Landai Sin*, or Little River, being applied to it by way of distinguishing it from the *Abba Sin*, or Indus. Both rivers, on entering the plain, form deltas, which are increased by artificial canals made for irrigation.

The valley of the Cabul river is naturally divided, by the mountain-ranges of the Lataband on the west and the Khaibar on the east, into three basins, called, from the principal towns in them, the Cabul, Jalalabad, and Peshawar basins.

The basin of Cabul includes a tract about thirty-six miles from east to west, and from eight to sixteen miles from north to south. This tract is again divided by two ridges of hills into three plains. The western plain, called Chahar-deh (or "Four villages") is about eight miles wide and twelve long. The town of Cabul stands at the base of a ridge of hills (called the Tak-i-shat) running from south to north, through which the Cabul river flows in a deep gorge. The Chahar-deh plain, which is to the west of this ridge, is very fertile, and abounds in fruit trees.

The eastern portion of the basin is wider, and is called Kohistan. On the west it is hemmed in by the Paghman Mountains, and on the north and east by the Hindu Kush. Its length is thirty miles, and average width seven miles. The western side of the plain of Kohistan is much higher than the eastern, along which flows the drainage of the opposite mountain. It is the favourite country residence of the Cabul inhabitants, and is thickly-studded with their strongly-built dwellings and well-cultivated gardens.

The plain of Logar is the third of the plains that are included in the upper basin of the Cabul river. It is about twenty miles wide from east to west, and about half that distance in length from north to south. Much of it is a swamp during part of the year, and it is surmised that the whole was at one time a lake. It is chiefly valuable as a grazing ground for the cattle, and especially the horses, of the Cabulese, but it also contains orchards and vineyards.

The Lataband Pass leads from the Cabul to the Jalalabad division of the valley. This mountainous region extends for about thirty miles, and numerous offsets reach it from the Safed Koh, leaving narrow valleys intervening. A series of steep ascents and descents is here met with, the ridges sometimes rising 1,000 or 1,500 feet above the valley, which are overhung with frowning boulders. To the south of this barren region is the Khurd Cabul Pass, through which runs the road from Cabul to Tazin and Jagdallak. At Jagdallak this road is joined by the road from Cabul through the Lataband Pass, which thence proceeds eastward through Gandamak to Jalalabad and Peshawar.

A marked change in the character of the valley of the Cabul river occurs at Gandamak, where the Jalalabad division of it may be said to begin. This extends from west to east about forty miles, and is on an average about ten miles wide. It is reached from Gandamak by a sudden descent from an elevation of 5,000 feet to one of 2,000. The description of the change given by the Emperor Baber has been often quoted :—"The moment you descend you see quite another world. The timber is different; its grains are of another sort; its animals are of a different species; and the manners and customs of its inhabitants are of a different kind." It is possible to leave the wheat harvest in progress at Jalalabad, and to find at Gandamak, only twenty-five miles distant, that it is but a few inches above the ground. "Here," exclaims one writer, "nature has planted the gates of India. The valleys of the upper basin, though still in the height of summer affected by a sun of fierce power, recall the climate and products of the finest part of temperate Europe; the region below is a chain of narrow, low, and hot plains, with climate and vegetation of an Indian character."

A narrow tract along the Cabul river is richly cultivated; beyond that on either side are barren wastes up to the foot of the hills, where village life and cultivation again appear. In April and May this region is visited by the same fierce hot winds that at this season prevail in the plains of India.

The Khaibar Pass leads from this central division of the Cabul basin to its most eastern portion, the plain of Peshawar, now British territory, but formerly, along with Sindh, an integral part of the Afghan dominions. It has been conjectured that down to a comparatively late date in the tertiary period a great inland lake filled up the deep basin of Peshawar, and even rose to a considerable height along the sides of the neighbouring hills, being fed by the Cabul and Swat rivers. It is supposed that in course of time the outlet by which the lake emptied its surplus stores into the Indus created a deep gorge through the rocky barrier that hemmed it in, and, step by step, the waters subsided to lower and yet lower levels, until at length the whole valley was drained of its overflowing flood, and became a mere circular glen, traversed by the united stream of the Cabul and the Swat, which had formerly filled its whole expanse. Yet even to the present day many signs of this primeval condition remain stamped indelibly upon the face of the Peshawar basin. Its bottom consists of a thick alluvial deposit, the relic of its ancient lacustrine state ; and through the yielding soil the rivers cut their way in numerous divergent channels, which still recall the memory of the almost forgotten lake. Especially in the rich wedge of land known as the Doab (*i.e.*, the tract between two rivers) do these numberless minor watercourses carry off and distribute the swollen current of the great mountain streams, thus preventing the possibility of inundation, and parcelling out the fertilising waters to the green fields around. In this way the Peshawar valley is freed from the danger of those two ever-present and alternative Indian curses,

Its Natural Features. 37

flood and famine, which usually succeed one another with such appalling rapidity during the wet and dry seasons respectively.

The fertility of the valley is so famous that the rice of Bara, grown along the banks of a stream bearing the same name, has the reputation throughout India of being food fit for princes.

The plain of Peshawar falls short of the Indus. Its elevation is 5,000 feet lower than the plain of Cabul, Peshawar itself being only 1,165 feet above the sea.

(II.) *The Central Table-land* is hardly more than twenty miles wide at its northern extremity, where it meets the plains of Maidan and the Logar river, which lies between it and the basin of Cabul. It widens in its length from N.E. to S.W., till at Ghazni it is nearly one hundred miles across, and this width is continued to its southern extremity, near Candahar. Its greatest elevation is reached at the Sher-i-dana Pass, north of Ghazni, and it slopes down on the northern side from 9,000 feet, near Ghazni, to less than 8,000 feet in the Maidan plain, and in the south it sinks towards Candahar as low as 3,500 feet. The variations of temperature experienced in this tract are, consequently, very great, ranging from a cold climate in the north to a comparatively hot one in the south. Thus Ghazni is very cold, and has a winter that lasts four or five months, during which hard frosts are experienced, the ice in the pools attaining a thickness of several feet even in a mild season. Candahar has, however, a temperate climate, with only slight frosts, and great heat in the summer, while the thermometer often varies as much as 40° between sunrise and three p.m. The rainfall here is small, and recourse has to be had to irrigation, for which ingenious methods are adopted. In the northern part good crops of barley and wheat are obtained by these means. The fruit of this region is considered inferior to that of Cabul. In the middle and southern tracts, occupied by the Ghilzais, a nomadic tribe, there is little cultivation, and that only near the large rivers, but pasture-grounds are numerous. Near Candahar, on the banks of the Argandab, wheat, rice, barley, and Indian corn are cultivated, and orchards are plentiful.

(III.) *The Upper Helmand Basin* is the tract to the north-west of the Central Table-land, and is the least-known tract of Afghanistan. The Helmand river (the classical *Etymander*) has its highest sources in the Koh-i-Baba and Paghman Mountains, between Cabul and Bamian. It exceeds the Cabul river in length, and probably also in volume. Its upper course is through the Hazarah country, and it is believed that for a course of nearly 300 miles this river has not been seen by a European. This un-

Its Natural Features. 39

known part of the river ends at Girishk, where the principal route from Candahar to Herat crosses it. From native sources of information it is gathered that the Helmand, until about forty miles above Girishk, has all the characteristics of a mountain stream. It receives its chief tributary, the Argandab (supposed to be the ancient *Arachotus*), about forty miles below Girishk, and here becomes a considerable stream, 300 yards wide and 9 feet deep. It continues fordable, however, to within 100 miles of its mouth. In its lower course the left bank is within a mile or so of the desert with its moving sands, but the vegetation on the banks is luxuriant. Cultivation seems to have fallen off from what it was in former times, the lower outlet appearing to have been the seat at some more or less remote period of a flourishing population.

Following generally a south-west course from its source till it enters Seistan, the Helmand there turns nearly northwards from a point situated a little to the north of 30° north latitude, and continues to flow in that direction to its outfall by several mouths in the lake of Seistan or Hamun (the ancient Aria Palus). The whole length is about 700 miles.

(IV.) *The Lower Helmand Basin* extends from the road leading from Girishk to Farrah on the north to the desert of Baluchistan on the south and south-east. On the west the plain of Seistan is its boundary, part of this plain being now included in the Persian kingdom.

(V.) *The Basin of the Herat River* lies between the Hazarah country on the east, and the Ghurian hills in Persian territory on the west. The Hari-rud or Herat river rises in the lofty Hazareh country, not far from the source of the Balkh river. For more than 100 miles its course is westward, at a height of many thousand feet above the sea. It then descends rapidly in the same direction to Aoba, where it begins to be used for irrigation. About sixty miles beyond this place it flows past Herat, at a distance of three miles south of the city. The Candahar road crosses the river near Herat by a masonry bridge of twenty-six arches. Numerous deep canals are here drawn off. The river turns north-west below Herat, and rapidly decreases in volume, owing to the immense stores taken from it for irrigation. It flows past Sarakhs, having previously received the Tejend or Mash-had stream, but accurate information of its further course is wanting. In a recent map the Tejend-rud (or Tejend river) is given as the main stream, into which the Hari-rud falls at Agha Derbend, fifty miles south of Sarakhs. Beyond that town a conjectural north-west course is indicated for the point of stream of at least 250 miles, and it is made to end in a lake called Lake Tejend, about fifty miles south of the ancient bed of the Oxus, on the borders of the Turkoman desert.

The plain of Herat is of considerable extent, and is covered with fortified villages, orchards, gardens, vineyards, and cornfields. The heat is excessive for two months, but the winter is cold, and snow falls in great quantities. South of Herat is the plain of Sabzawar, thirty miles long and twenty wide, and partly cultivated. This plain and the Anandara to the south of it are watered by the Harut-rud, and the canals drawn from it. This river, besides receiving a considerable affluent, the Khushkak, or Khushrudak, forms a true delta with fifteen branches. The Harut-rud has a course of about 250 miles to its outfall in the Lake of Seistan. It has been confounded with the Hari-rud, or river of Herat, which has led, perhaps, to the long-prevalent mistake that the latter flowed south into the Seistan Lake.

(VI.) *The Eastern Portion of the Table-land* is very little known, as it has been rarely visited by Europeans. It is believed to be little cultivated, and to be occupied by nomadic tribes, of whom the Ghilzais in the north, the Kakars in the south, and the Vaziris in the east, are the principal. The Gomal river drains the northern part, but rarely reaches the Indus except in times of flood. This region may be said to extend from the Suliman Mountains to the watershed between the tributaries of the Indus on the east and the Helmand on the west respectively. This watershed is a ridge about 1,000 feet above the table-land, and is known by several names, such as the Jadran Mountains in the north, and the Kohnak, Kand, and Kapar Mountains in the centre and south.

(VII.) *The Northern Mountain regions of the Hazarah and Eimak* occupy, together with the Koh-i-Baba, the whole country between 34° and 36° N. lat., and between 68° and 63" E. long., covering an area of about 50,000 square miles. The climate of the northern part is very severe on account of its high elevation, and the Hazarahs are obliged to cut great quantities of grass for their sheep, which, during three months of the winter, are generally housed under the same roof with their owners. The country of the Hazarahs has an average elevation of 10,000 feet. In the Eimak country the elevation of the mountains is less, and the general level is also lower. During the heats of summer pastures are sought here by the Durani tribes, who come up from the plains below, where all the grass is completely burnt up in that season.

(VIII.) *The Southern Table-land* is the tract between the Khoja Amran range and the Mari and Bagti Mountains, and consists of the valley of the river Lora, and the country of Thal. This river from the Pishni valley westward is unknown, and, although it is usually considered to belong to the Helmand basin, it has not been ascertained that its waters ever reach that river. It rises near the Kand and Joba peaks in an offset of the Suliman Mountains, and flows westward. The greater part of the Khoja Amran range is unknown, as, indeed, are the upper courses of the Arghasan and Kadani streams, which join the Dori, a confluent of the Argandab.

Besides these main natural divisions of Afghanistan Proper, the Khanates of Afghan Turkestan and Badakhshan are included in the Afghan dominions, as the former are subject, and the latter tributary, to the Amir of Cabul. Afghan Turkestan includes the Khanates of Kunduz, Khulm, Balkh, with Akcha; the western Khanates of Sir-i-pul, Shibrghan, Andkhui, and Maimana, which are known as the "Four Domains" (Chiliar Wilayat); and such of the Hazarah tribes as lie to the north of the Hindu Kush and the Paropamisan chain. This tract includes the whole southern half of the Oxus basin, from the Kokcha to the Murghab river.

Between the district of Swat and the dependencies of Badakhshan and Kunduz, and in the heart of the hill-country beyond the Indian frontier, lies the interesting tract called Kafiristan, or the land of the Kafirs (the term used by Muhammadans for all who have not embraced Islam). Roughly speaking, it may be defined as the country that lies on the eastern slopes of the Hindu Kush, from the Valley of Panjkir, near Cabul, and as far north as Mastoj and Chitral, or Kashkar.

RIVERS.

The chief are the Cabul, Helmand, Harut, Harirud, Gomal, and Lora, with their tributaries, which have, perhaps, been sufficiently described in the preceding pages.

The Kuram river rises in the Safed Koh Mountains, and drains the southern slopes of the Salt Range. The upper part of its valley is known as the Bangash-i-bala, or Upper Bangash, and the lower part descends gradually to the Indus, forming the plain of Bannu. This plain, as well as the tract called Danian, which lies south of Bannu and to the east of the Suliman Mountains as far as Mittan-Kot, is included in British territory.

The rivers of Afghan Turkestan and Badakhshan are mostly tributaries of the Oxus, which forms the boundary of these provinces as far as Khoja Salih ferry. The Kokcha, or river of Badakhshan, is famous for the mines of lapis lazuli in its neighbourhood. The Kunduz river has its chief source in the Bamian stream, and just where the latter receives a confluent from the Hajihak Pass, extensive ruins are found, the name of which, Zohak, connects them with the most ancient legends of Persian history.

The Khulm, Balkh, and Murghab are the other chief rivers of this part of the Afghan dominions; and they have numerous tributaries. The last is known to reach Merv, and is then lost in the desert.

LAKES.

Besides the Lora Hamun, the name given to the lake in which the Lora river is supposed to end, a small part of the Lake of Seistan or Zarah is included in Afghanistan; and there is also a salt lake called the Ab-i-istada (standing water) on the Ghilzai plateau. This last is about forty miles in circuit, and very shallow, nowhere, perhaps, exceeding twelve feet in depth. The chief feeder is the Ghazni river, but the waters of the lake itself are so salt and bitter, that fish entering them sicken and die. The dreary and barren aspect of the shores of this lake is said to rival that of the shores of the Dead Sea.

PROVINCES AND TOWNS.

The present political divisions of Afghanistan are not known with accuracy, but they probably consist of Cabul, Herat, Ghazni, Candahar, Jalalabad, Afghan Turkestan, and the Hazarah division.

Besides Cabul, Herat, Ghazni, Candahar, and Jalalabad, there are few places of such importance as to deserve the name of towns. Istalif, Charikar, Kala't-i-Ghilzai, and Girishk, are all places connected with our former occupation of Afghanistan, at some of which British troops were stationed.

Farrah and Sabzawar, in the west, are places of some importance, from a military point of view. Zarni, to the east of Herat, is noted for the ruins in its neighbourhood, supposed to be those of the ancient capital of Ghor, the seat of a monarchy which supplanted the Ghaznavites, and obtained extensive dominion in the twelfth and thirteenth centuries. The rule of the Ghori Kings extended at one time over Khorasan, Afghanistan, Sindh, and Lahore.

Kunduz, the capital of an old Khanate, is a mere collection of mud huts. Balkh, the ancient Bactra (of which no certain trace remains), is now entirely deserted for another site, Taktapul, eight miles east of the old city. Akcha, the capital of a recently-conquered Uzbek Khanate, is a fortified town, with a citadel.

The chief towns in the "Four Domains" are Shibrghan (12,000 inhabitants), Andkhui, Maimana, and Sir-i-pul.

Having now completed our rapid survey of the natural features of Afghanistan, we pass on to consider the climate, productions, and commerce of the country, which form the subject of the next chapter.

CHAPTER II.

AFGHANISTAN—ITS CLIMATE AND PRODUCTIONS.

Variations in Climate—Mineral Wealth—Vegetable Kingdom—Agriculture —Irrigation—Animal Kingdom—Domestic Animals—Industry and Commerce—Trade Routes—Povindahs.

CLIMATE.

THE diversity of climate found in Afghanistan, of which frequent mention has been made in the preceding pages, is due to difference of elevation rather than of latitude. So severe are the winters at Ghazni (7,730 feet) that the people stay in their houses nearly all the winter. Indeed, if tradition is to be credited, the entire population has perished in former times from severe snow-storms. On the other hand, the summer heat, except in the very elevated parts of the Hindu Kush and other high mountains, is everywhere very great. The southwestern portion of the country is exposed during the summer to a deadly hot wind, which renders the whole country a sandy and almost uninhabited desert. Ferrier says that at Herat the wind blows constantly from May to September from the north-west, and its violence is equal to prostrating houses, uprooting trees, and other similar devastation. The summer heat in the province of Candahar is intense, and in Seistan almost unbearable. The rains of the south-west monsoon reach the eastern border of the Afghan table-land, but owing to the distance from the sea they are scanty, and last only for a month, from the middle of July to the middle of August. They do not extend beyond Jalalabad in the valley of the Cabul river, but they fall at the head of the Kuram valley. They are not experienced to the west of the Suliman range.

In the higher regions the summer is dry, rain not falling from May to September or October, and being rare in November.

The winter rains are the most considerable, and are accompanied with falls of snow, while sleet falls with the spring rains in the valley of the Cabul river.

Herat is credited with a milder climate, the most agreeable, it is said, in Asia. The temperature, says Ferrier, rarely exceeds 91° to 93° (Fahr.), and was never more than 98° while he was there. The winter, too, is so mild that only in one year out of four is there enough ice to enable it to be stored.

The Emperor Baber, speaking of the extent to which change of climate can be obtained near Cabul by change of place, says that at one day's journey from that city you may find a place where snow never falls, and, at two hours' journey, a place where snow never melts!

Some local climates are much lauded by the Afghans for healthiness and comfort, such as the Toba hills and some valleys of the Safed Koh range of mountains.

PRODUCTIONS.

The knowledge we have of the geology of Afghanistan is meagre; but there seems reason to believe that the mineral wealth of the country is great, although little utilised. Dr. Lord, who was with the army of occupation in 1839, remarks that antimony, iron, and lead are found in the Ghorband valley, and marble quarries in the hills near Maidan.

According to a Russian authority, the hills south-west of Cabul and the Hazarah districts are the richest in mineral wealth.

Gold (on the same authority) is found in the rivulets of Paghman, in the rivers Cabul, Kunar, and their tributaries. The principal places where gold is washed down on the Cabul river are said to be Jalalabad and Michni; on the Kunar, Chachar-Bag, Peshat, and Kirch. It is believed that all the rivers coming from the western side of the Hindu Kush are auriferous. Silver, formerly mined in large quantities in Kohistan, is now only gathered in the valley of Ghorband. Lead occurs in the Hazarah district north of Candahar, and in the Ghorband valley. Of copper, there are large quantities in the Gal Koh hills, in the territory of the Jaguri tribe of the Hazarah. Here there is also antimony, which is also met with north of Candahar, and in the Khaibar hills. Sulphur, saltpetre, and salammoniac may be dug out of the Ghorband and Jaguri territories. Iron is abundant along the western slopes of the Hindu Kush. There are mines in the valley of the Panjkora, and in the hills west of Bunnu, whence the article is exported to India. Iron works also exist in Badakhshan, near Faizabad, and in Southern Cabul, near Kaniguram. The iron, being entirely smelted with charcoal, is highly valued in the adjoining countries.

Coal is said to be found in places between the Upper Kuram and the Gomal valleys. Nitre is abundant in the soil, all over the south-west of Afghanistan, and affects the water of the subterranean canals, called "Karez," which are made for purposes of irrigation. Salt is found in ample quantities in the Salt Range, a chain of low hills, that do not rise more than 2,000 feet above the level of the Indus, and extend from its western bank W.N.W. to the Suliman Mountains, which they touch a few miles south of the Safed Koh. The chief workings of this rock-salt are at Kalabagh, on the Indus, whence it is exported to different parts of Upper India.

VEGETABLE KINGDOM.

From Dr. Bellew's interesting Journal, and other works, an exhaustive account of the distribution of vegetation on the mountains of Afghanistan can be obtained. Vegetation is almost entirely absent from the distant and terminal prolongation of the great mountain chains; but there is abundant growth of forest trees, and, indeed, every form of vegetation on the main ranges and their larger off-shoots.

On the Safed Koh and its immediate branches, we have abundant growth of large forest-trees, at a height of 6,000 to 10,000 feet, among which are enumerated *Cedrus deodara*, *Abies excelsa*, *Pinus longifolia*, *P. Pinaster*, the edible pine, and the larch. The yew, hazel, juniper, walnut, wild peach, and almond are also found. Under these grow the rose, honeysuckle, gooseberry, currant, hawthorn, rhododendron, and a greensward of the richest kind. The lemon and wild-vine are commoner on the northern mountains.

Down to 3,000 feet the wild-olive, rock-rose, wild-privet, acacias, and mimosas, barberry, and *zizyphus* are met with. To the eastward *Chamærops*, *Bignonia*, *shisham*, *Salvadora persica*, *verbena*, and *acanthus* are found. The scanty vegetation on the terminal ridges is mostly herbal, with rare and stunted shrubs ; but many of them are naked rocks. Ferns and mosses are confined to the lofty ranges.

The rue and wormwood found among the low brushwood of the dreary plains south of Herat are used as domestic medicines, the former for rheumatism and neuralgia, the latter in fever, debility, and dyspepsia, as well as for a vermifuge. The rue, owing to its nauseous odour, is believed to drive away evil spirits.

Planted by the hand of man are such trees as the mulberry, willow, poplar, ash, and plane, found only in cultivated districts. The gum-resin of Western Afghanistan (Candahar and Herat) is a valuable article of commerce, being used in India as a condiment. Edible rhubarb is mentioned as a great luxury. It grows wild in the hills, and is eaten both raw and cooked. *Sanjit* and *salep* are names of an edible fruit and root exported to India. The pistachio-nut is found in the extreme north. Mushrooms and similar fungi are largely consumed. There are two kinds of manna sold ; one, *turanjbin*, is taken from the camel-thorn and dwarf tamarisk ; the other, *sar-kasht*, from a tree called "black-wood" (siyah chob) by the natives.

The fruit of the mulberry-tree, of which there are as many as twelve varieties, is ground into a flour, and forms an important article of food in the country near the Hindu Kush. Some individuals possess as many as 10,000 trees. A tree of the best kind will sometimes bear 800 lbs. of mulberries, and taking a third of this as the average produce, a larger population could be supported by it than by tillage. Silk is not produced to any great extent, and only in a few places.

AGRICULTURE.

So far as is known, the land belongs to local chieftains, who, while letting it to vassals, themselves have to pay a tribute to their suzerains. Only on the well-watered banks of rivers and canals, where agriculture attains to some degree of perfection, is the land owned or rented by individuals. Pastures are always the common property of the clans, steppes being considered nobody's property. Like all other rights and personal possessions, title-deeds are worth but little in Afghanistan. Everybody's hand being against everybody, landed proprietors are frequently expelled, or else expelling others, to transfer themselves to fresh scenes. Some emigrate to neighbouring Khanates, and by dint of the strong arm manage to establish themselves on ground belonging to another clan.

Speaking generally, there are in Afghanistan, as in India, two harvests, the spring (*babarak*) sown in October and reaped in April, consisting of wheat, barley, and lentils; and the autumnal (*tirmai*), sown in April or May and reaped in September, of which rice, millet and vorghum, maize (*Phascolus Mungo*), tobacco, beet, and turnips are the chief crops. The higher districts have, however, but one harvest.

In consequence of the difference of climate in various parts of the country, agriculture is by no means the same thing in the north as in the south. In Cabul the land is well-watered by canals, and very fertile. In the valley of the river Cabul, from the Khaibar hills to the capital, there is no barren, unproductive soil. Arable land in those parts is so extremely valuable that—a rare thing in Afghanistan —it is amply provided with roads. There are here plenty of ariks or open canals, not to speak of the underground rills, artificially laid down in some parts. These water-courses are constructed by the Government or village authorities, or by charitable individuals wishing to confer a benefit upon their neighbours. In the case of Government waterworks, a tax has to be paid for their use; whereas, village canals are frequently the joint property of the community.

The kind of subterranean canal called "Karez," which enables the water of a hill or rising ground to be brought out at its foot in a rivulet, so as to be disposed of at the pleasure of the cultivator, is common in the tracts to the south of Ghazni, where the rainfall is small, and the rivers of small volume. The mode of their construction is thus described:— At the spot where it is wished that the water shall issue, a well is dug; and above it, in the acclivity, another is made at the distance of five to twenty yards. Other wells are made above at similar distances from each other, the highest being made the deepest, so that its bottom may be slightly above the level of that of the one below, and so on. When as many wells have been thus made as the farmer can afford, or thinks necessary, a subterranean passage is burrowed from the lowest, joining the bottom of each well, and the water rushes forth in such force sometimes as to be able to turn a mill. Some of these *Kareses* extend to two or more miles—a celebrated one near Ghazni, ascribed to Sultan Mahmud, being said to be thirty miles long, including offsets.

In the Kafiristan Mountains agriculture ascends to a considerable height, wherever an arable plot is to be found. In other parts, where corn cannot be sown, the hills are planted with fruit trees in terraces. The harvest in these parts principally depends upon the amount of rainfall.

South of the Safed Koh hills, in the district of Kuram, agriculture is confined to the valley of the Kuram, which in some parts is twenty-two miles wide. In this valley, as in all other valleys of East

Afghanistan, there is a stony ledge of ground at the foot of the hills unfit for agriculture. The mountains have plenty of arable land that cannot be cultivated for want of rain or wells. Still, further south, in the district occupied by the Mahsud Waziri tribe, the cultivated land forms only two or three per cent. of the entire area; the rest being barren for want of water. The few fields there are close to the rivers, where they enjoy the benefit of an occasional inundation.

The Logar and Ghazni districts, in the far west of Cabul, are well cultivated, and supply corn to the whole Principality.

In Candahar, from the source of the river Tarnak (a tributary of the Argandab), to the capital, the country offers but scanty opportunity for agriculture. Fields, as a rule, follow the river-bank in narrow strips, or sometimes cluster round water-courses, mostly subterranean in those parts; nor is the lower valley of the Tarnak much more productive. A more cheerful aspect is offered by the Helmand valley, having fields and gardens to about a mile and a-half to two miles on either bank, as far as the Seistan Lake. South of the Helmand, the desert appears rather unexpectedly. North of the river, however, stretching away to the hills, it is here and there studded with villages surrounded by oases with artificial irrigation.

Herat, possessing a good soil traversed by several rivers, is considered the most fertile part of the plateau of Afghanistan. Here the harvests are uniformly good, yielding forty-fold. The district of Ghorband is the storehouse of the country; and such is the superabundance of land, that where corn might be grown cattle are frequently pastured. Every now and then the country is the scene of Persian warfare, which prevents the development of agriculture.

Seistan, the basin of Lake Hamun, and of the deltas of surrounding rivers, is a plain intersected by low ridges. Two-thirds of the surface is sand, the remaining third being alluvial soil, capable of high cultivation, but mostly occupied by tamarind trees. The delta of the Helmand, with its many parallel water-courses, is very fertile, and wholly under the plough. The fields are here separated by quick-set hedges; the harvests are abundant, and much is exported.

Of the Turkestan Khanates under Afghan control Balkh is the most productive, thanks to its extensive system of irrigation. Notwithstanding political troubles, and the consequent decrease of the population, Balkh still yields enough to supply some of the neighbouring Principalities. The valley of Kunduz, though fertile, is swampy, and has an unhealthy climate, compelling people to live in the hill districts. All attempts at agriculture have failed, colonists invariably succumbing to malaria.

There is a deal of arable, well-irrigated ground in the other Khanates; but they are too frequently exposed to war and robbery to permit of the labour of the husbandman. In all these parts plenty of good land lies fallow.

The agricultural produce of Afghanistan is very various. Wheat, maize, barley, and millet form the principal food of the population. Rice requiring much water is only planted in the valleys of the tributaries of the Indus, in Kunduz, Balkh, and some localities of Herat. Every variety of fruit known in Europe grows well, the rhubarb being especially fine. Indeed, fruit is one of the great staples of food in the country, and a principal article of exportation. The Cabul valley gardens are famous for peaches, apricots, cherries, apples, pears, pomegranates, figs, and quince; the Jalalabad valley has also lemons and dates. The white mulberry-tree is found everywhere; the other species with red fruit is also there. It has been mentioned already that the mulberries themselves are dried, ground into flour, and made into cakes, either with or without corn-flour. Pistachio-nuts are grown in such quantities in the neighbourhood of Maimana that they are exported in caravans to Persia and Bagdad. It is a peculiarity of the climate that all these excellent comestibles get ripe at a considerable altitude. Pomegranates flourish at 4,500 feet above the sea, while apricots ascend to 8,000 feet, and mulberries to 9,000 feet. Grapes are plentiful, and the making of wine is a chief branch of industry, especially in Kafiristan. Considerable quantities of grapes are dried and eaten as raisins. Some sorts are gathered before they are ripe, and exported to Bombay, and other parts of India. In Herat a special tax is imposed upon the manufacture of wine, which can only be carried on by Government licence. Tobacco is much grown and used. The three most approved growths in East Afghanistan are the Candahar, Balkh, and Mansurabad, of which the last is the best. In Herat there are two tobacco harvests in the year, the first being accounted the best. There is little cotton produced in the country, except in the Bangash district, near the Indian frontier; but this, too, is indifferent in quality and quantity. Of other plants we may mention the madder, in Candahar and Ghazni, much employed for dyeing woollen cloth, and also exported; Indian hemp used in brewing a narcotic beverage; a species of rhubarb, producing oil for lamps; assafœtida, a shrub encountered everywhere, but more especially in the south, from which pitch is extracted. This pitch, used in Afghanistan for medical purposes only, is frequently exported to India. A decoction made from the young leaves is drunk by the Afghans and Baluchis in Seistan.

ANIMAL KINGDOM.

The tiger is found in the north-eastern hill country. The leopard, panther, hyæna, the wolf (said sometimes to attack single horsemen in the wilder tracts), wild dog, and small Indian fox are more or less common. Bears of two Himalayan species are met with. Wild sheep, Indian deer, especially the *bara singha*, the wild hog, and the wild ass, are found. No elephant or rhinoceros has been traced within many hundred miles of Afghanistan; but they formerly existed in the Peshawar plain. Only one species of bird is known to be peculiar to the country; but vast numbers of birds of Indian and desert forms flock to it in the breeding season. Among reptiles a tortoise peculiar to Afghanistan has been discovered. Our knowledge of the zoology of the country is confessedly fragmentary and imperfect in the extreme.

Of domestic animals the most important are the sheep, of which there are two kinds, both having the broad, fat tail, which in some parts of the Eimak Mountains is said to be of such a size that a small cart is put under the tail. They are the chief property of the Hazarah and Eimak tribes, who live

Its Climate and Productions. 61

chiefly by selling wool and woollen stuffs. The sheep on the mountains give two fleeces, the spring one being coarser than the autumn one. Mutton is the principal animal food of the people. The goats, generally of a black variety, seem to be of an inferior breed, except in the higher ranges of the Koh-i-Baba and Paropamisan Mountains.

Cattle-breeding here, as in the steppes and hills of Russian Asia, requires in this climate a frequent change of pasture. Thus the Ghilzae, Afridi, and other clans pass the summer in the Safed Koh hills, descending for the winter to the plain of Candahar and the Indus valley, and sometimes crossing the frontier into British territory. The Baluchis nomadise in summer near the river Helmand; but in autumn, with the first frost, may be seen wandering to the southern steppes, where water is found only at that season. Excepting in the Cabul valley, cattle breeding is carried on in all parts of Afghanistan by a nomad population, living side by side with the sedentary and agricultural inhabitants. The nomads rarely apply themselves to agricultural pursuits. Of the domestic animals, camels, dromedaries, and a cross between the two, are used for riding and draught, as well as for the milk and butter they yield; their flesh is only eaten by the very poorest. The clan Gesarai, living in the hills where camels are of little use, value them, however, for their wool.

Cabul has few camels, and only a cart-horse sort of horse. The species of horse called yabu is employed for draught in the hills. A finer breed is seen among the Hazarahs, in the Khanate of Maimana. In the south, the breeding and sale of horses are almost exclusively in the hands of the Baluchis; but a peculiarly valuable kind introduced by Nadir Shah from Persia is only met with among the Afghan tribe.

The cows of Candahar and Seistan are said to give very large quantities of milk.

Dog-breeding is pursued with advantage, owing to the favourable climate.

The so-called "Persian" cats in reality chiefly come from Afghanistan.

INDUSTRY AND COMMERCE.

The industrial products of Afghanistan are confined to a little silk, chiefly used in domestic manufacture; carpets from Herat, some of which are soft, brilliant, and durable, and pass in India for "Persian" carpets; felts and woven goods made from the wool of the sheep, goats, and Bactrian camel; sheepskins; and rosaries made from chrysolite.

The manufactures of Afghanistan include a list of the simplest trades of semi-civilised life, such as jewellers, gold and silver smiths, sellers of armour, sellers of bows and arrows, sellers of glass ornaments for women, confectioners, tobacconists, embroiderers, and such like. To these are added a few booksellers and bookbinders. The inhabitants of the Eimak and Hazarah Mountains do not export their wool, but manufacture it into carpets, grain-bags, rugs, &c. As there are few, if any, navigable rivers in Afghanistan, nor any wheeled carriage, the mode of conveyance of goods is by beasts of burden, chiefly camels, though mules and asses are largely used in the mountainous districts. The principal trade of India with Western Asia and Europe has from time immemorial been by sea; yet large and valuable caravans at one time carried Indian products into Persia, Turkestan, and China by the four lines of communication that pass through or near Afghan territory. The most northern leads from Leh in Ladakh to Yarkand in Chinese Turkestan, and is the most difficult and dangerous. The second passes through Lahore, Peshawar, the Khaibar Pass, to Cabul, where it divides into two roads, one passing over the Bamian and other passes into Afghan Turkestan, and the other running through Ghazni to Candahar, where it meets the two southern lines. These last are divergent portions of the third line which passes through the Gomal Pass from Dera Ismail Khan, and divides on the tableland into two roads, one running to Cabul and the other to Ghazni and Candahar. The fourth road begins at Karachi, follows the Indus to Shikarpur, diverges thence to the north-west, and passes through the Bolan Pass into the valley of Shal. It continues through Quettah to Candahar. From Candahar the joint road passes westward across the Helmand, through Farrah, Sabzawar, and Herat, to Mash-had in Persia, and thence to Tcheran, the capital. From Herat to Merv and Bokhara is another trade route. The Syads of Herat, who are large horsedealers, used to carry on a considerable trade in slaves, getting their chief victims from the Hazarahs, whom they sold to the Turkomans. A large traffic in wool has of late years sprung up from the regions west of the Indus, some millions of pounds being annually shipped from Karachi, the port of Sindh.

The *Povindahs*, a class of merchants that are the representatives of the oldest Asiatic traders, carry on traffic between India, Khorasan, and Bokhara, by means of long strings of camels and ponies banded in large, armed caravans. They battle their way twice a-year between Bokhara and the Indus, bullying, fighting, evading, or bribing the hostile and marauding foes in their path. It is interesting to observe how these ancient traders accommodate themselves to modern conditions of commerce, They cannot pass armed through British territory, so they quietly deposit their weapons at the Indus. Leaving their camels and families in the plains of the Panjab, they take their goods by rail to the great cities of Hindustan, and even penetrate as far as Bombay and Rangoon. In March they return to their families, and back again to the Ghilzai Tableland, whence they despatch caravans again to Cabul Bokhara, and other cities in Western Asia.

CHAPTER III.

THE PEOPLE, LANGUAGE, LITERATURE, AND ANTIQUITIES OF AFGHANISTAN.

The Afghans, Pathans, or Pushtanahs—Division into Tribes—Non-Afghan Population—Estimated Population—Russian Account—Supposed Jewish Origin—Kafirs—Sir John Kaye's Description of the Afghans—Language and Literature—Judicial Institutions—Military System—Russian Account of the Afghan Army—Antiquities.

ALTHOUGH the country derives its name from the Afghans, these people are but a portion—barely half, it is conjectured—of the total inhabitants. According to some authorities, the name Afghan is not applied to any tribe by its own members; but the better opinion seems to be that the Afghans, or Pathans, or Pushtanahs, as they are variously called, include a large number of tribes, of which the most important are the following:—

(1.) *Durani* or Abdali, to which Ahmad Shah belonged. They dwell in the south and south-west.

(2). *Ghilzai*, the strongest and bravest, said to be identical with the Khiliji dynasty of Delhi kings of the tenth and eleventh centuries.

(3.) *Yusufzai*, a turbulent race, dwelling partly in

the British district of Peshawar, and partly as an independent tribe in the hill country north of the Khaibar.

(4.) *Kakars*, chiefly independent, in the south-east of Afghanistan, near Baluchistan.

The non-Afghan population consists of numerous tribes, among which the *Tajiks* and *Kazlbashis* include the most industrious of all the inhabitants of Afghanistan. The *Hazarahs* are supposed to be of Mongol or *Mughal* origin, and pay tribute to the Afghans only when compelled. These people are said to be notorious for loose domestic morals, like the ancient *Massagetæ* who occupied their mountains. They are found all over Afghanistan as menial servants, and are, or were, often sold as slaves. *Eimak* is the name given to a nomadic tribe dwelling near the *Hazaras*. *Hindkis*, or people of Hindu descent, *Jats*, and *Baluchis*, are names of other tribes. Colonel Macgregor makes the following estimate of the population:—

Afghan Turkestan	642,000
Chitralis and Kafirs	150,000
Emiaks and Hazarahs	400,000
Tajiks	500,000
Kazlbashis	150,000
Hindkis and Jats	500,000
Kohistanis	200,000
Afghans and Pathans (including 400,000 independent Yusufzais, &c.)	2,359,000
	4,901,000

The Russian Military Department sets down the total population of Afghanistan at 6,000,000, occupying an area of 10,000 geographical square miles. The sparsity of the population on this estimate may be concluded from the fact that Germany on the same area supports over 40,000,000 people. An attempt has also been made by the Russian Military Department to estimate the population of each province and district, but as these figures are admittedly conjectural to the last degree, we will not burden our pages by quoting them.

The very elaborate account of the races and tribes which has been published by the same department deserves more attention. It states the number of distinct races to be nine—Afghans, Tajiks, Kazlbashis, Hazaris, Usbeks, Hindus, Jats, Kafirs, and Arabs.

The Afghans are said to number about 3,000,000, and to be divided into five tribes, and these again to be subdivided into 405 clans (khail), each of which includes numerous families. Of the 405 clans, 277 call themselves Afghans, and the remaining 128 prefer the patronymic of Pathan. All boast of deriving their descent from the Ten Tribes of Israel, their own chroniclers calling the Afghans *Bani-Israel* (Arabic for Sons of Israel). They claim to be the offspring of King Saul, through a son whom they ascribe to him named Jeremiah, who again had a son named Afghana. The descendants of Afghana were, accord-

People, Language, and Antiquities. 69

ing to the legend, removed by Nebuchadnezzar, and found their way to the mountains north of Herat. They embraced the faith of Muhammad, by their own showing, nine years after the prophet's announcement of his mission. The earliest written statement of this story dates from the sixteenth century. We cannot enter at any length into the arguments which have been advanced in favour of the Jewish origin of the Afghans. The most weighty appears to be the facial resemblance they bear to the Jews; but this is shared by the inhabitants of Cashmere, the Tajiks, and other Asiatics.

Though spread over the whole country, the bulk of the Afghan population live in the eastern and south-eastern provinces, being inveterate mountaineers, and preferring the lofty hills on the Indian frontier to any more profitable and convenient residence. Of those living in the adjoining valleys some are in the habit of nomadising on British territory part of the year.

The principal clans in the north-east are the *Shinwari*, north of Cabul, almost independent; the *Tarkalanai*, in the south-western basin of the Panjkora, capable of sending 10,000 men into the field; the *Yusufzai*, divided into two branches, having separate khans and about 70,000 fighting men, whose country has already been indicated; the *Utman Khels* on the left bank of the Cabul river, who muster 10,000 fighting men; and the Upper Momunds.

South of the Cabul river in Cabulistan and the Panjab hills, lining the Indus valley, the Tarnokhi muster 6,000 fighting men. The Afridi, the most numerous of the border tribes, spending the greater part of the year on the Cabul hills, and descending only in summer into the Indus valley, glory in the possession of 15,000 armed men. To them belong the Khaibar and Shinvari people, famous for their martial and savage characteristics. Protected by the Khaibar hills, they are entirely independent, and receive from 10,000 to 20,000 rupees a year from the Cabul Government as a consideration for allowing caravans to pass. Some thirty years ago there were counted some 20,000 armed men in and near the Khaibar Pass. The Khaibar men are divided into many sections, each of them having a separate Khan and refusing to acknowledge any superior authority. Among the more prominent branches of the Afridi, the Jawaki, the Zaka-Khel, the Galli, and the Adam Khail deserve to be mentioned. The Lower Momund (12,000 armed men) occupy the south-western corner of the district of Peshawar. The strip of land separating the British districts of Peshawar and Kohat takes its name from the Khattak, who, notwithstanding their 15,000 warriors, lead a pacific agricultural life. The Orakzai inhabit the Ganga valley south-west of Kohat, and the Tirak valley. West of them there are the Bangash, in the valley of the Miranzai and part of the Kuram valley, within the boundaries of Cabul. South of the Kuram valley, between the districts of Bannu and Tank, the country is infested by the robber tribes of the Batani (5,000 fighting-men), living partly on English, partly on Cabul territory. The Suliman hills (Takhti Suliman, *Anglicè* the Throne of Solomon), in the south-eastern extremity of Afghanistan, harbours the three martial brotherhoods of the Shirani, Ushterani, and Kazrani. The Shirani, 10,000 armed men, make constant inroads into the valleys, and up to the pacification of the country by the English were the terror of the whole region. They live in the direction of Dera Ismail Khan. The Kazrani have about 5,000 rifles and are less warlike.

West of these, and still included in the Cabul frontiers, there is the extensive district of Daur, reaching from the river Gomal to the river Kuram, and inhabited by the Vezir people, divided into the three branches of the Makhsud, the Vezir in the south, the Derveshkhel in the centre, and the Kabulkhel in the north. The Vezir are a powerful and independent race, mostly nomads, leading a pastoral life, staying in the hills in summer; the winter entices them down to the Indus valley.

Their principal centres are the towns of Kaniguram and Makin. The upper valley of the Kuram is inhabited by the Turi and Jaji, of the Pathan division of the people. Further down the valley we meet with a portion of the Zaimakht, whose principal mass reside south-west. The mountainous district of Khost, south of the Kuram, is the property of small hill tribes—the Driplara, the Drikuti, Mattun, Gurbus, Torzai, and others.

The powerful clan of the Ghilzai or Ghilji, with numerous sub-divisions, are the owners of the Kilat-i-Ghilzai region. Their southern frontier is formed by the Durani country, which extends to Candahar. In the environs of Candahar and Ghazni there are also the Ashaksai and Nurzai, and others whose territories are less clearly divided.

Of the branches of the Afghan people living in the western parts of the kingdom we know but little. The most numerous are the Berduran. The Barakzai to whom belongs the Khan, have 60,000 families, and accordingly are one of the strongest Afghan tribes.

Next to the Afghans, the Tajiks are the most numerous race in the country. They are the aboriginal element in the Western Provinces, and, being a sedentary people, are called Tajik—*i.e.*, peasants, in contradistinction to the Turk or warrior. They are now divided into a sedentary portion calling themselves Parsivan or Parsi Zuban (that is, Persian speaking), and nomads known as Eimaks. The latter wander about in the hills surrounding the upper basin of the Hari-rud, and are mixed up with the Turkish tribes who immigrated under Jengis and Timur. Of these mixed tribes we know the Char Eimak, the Jamshedi, the Firoz Kuzi, Taimuni or Tegmuni, and the Zuri. Cognate to them are the Timurs, formed by Timur Shah out of the heterogeneous mob of his camp towards the end of the last century. The Taimuns are settled in the three districts of Teivere, Darya Dere, and Devaza, each having a separate Khan. Up to 1844, when the ruler of Herat transplanted 45,000 to the country adjoining his capital, they were estimated at 10,000 souls. The Taimun territory is situated on the southern declivity of the Sakh Kug hills, and was anciently called Gur. The Zuri is an insignificant clan. The Firoz Kuzi formerly lived further west in Persian Khorasan, but were transferred by Timur to their present settlement in Herat. They are now divided into five branches with five chiefs living in the forts of Kades, Darzi, Kuche, Chicharan, and Daulat Yar, situated in the upper valleys of the Hari-rud and Murghab. Kades was subjugated in 1844 by the Hazarah, but the other branches remained independent. The Zuri and Jamshedi, formerly potent and respected, now occupy the small territory in the

Murghab, to which they emigrated in the heroic period of Persian history. Their Khan resides at Bala Murghab, whence many raids are undertaken into neighbouring lands. The sedentary portion of the Tajiks are numerously represented only in Cabul Kohistan, in the valleys of Ghorband, Panjshir, and Nijaur, where they amounted to 40,000 families at the beginning of this century. They are warlike, almost entirely independent, and divided into small fraternities under the direction of special Khans. The Tajik branch in Logar, 8,000 families strong, is distinguished for its bravery. In the other parts of Afghanistan the Tajiks are more or less mixed up with the Afghans, living sometimes in Afghan villages, sometimes in separate colonies, under the direction of Ketkhuds or Elders. In these parts they have no landed property, but rent land from the Afghans, and altogether occupy a very inferior position. In the towns they are a gentle, hardworking race, and take to trades which the Afghans despise; in the villages they are justly famous for the excellence of their husbandry. Many of these Cabul Tajiks serve in the Anglo-Indian forces, where they are called Turks, and enjoy a good character. The Tajiks also form the original population of the Badakhshan region, where they are divided into the three groups of Raman, Shagnan, and Vashan. John Wood regarded the Chitral and Kafir people also as

Tajiks; but these being undoubtedly of different extraction, the Persian origin of the Badakshan Tajiks must appear very problematic.

The third race are the Kazlbashi, transferred by Nadir Shah from Persia to Cabul in 1737. They are a medley of Persians and Turks, of the Jevanshir, Afshar, and Muradshahi tribes, who speak Persian, and, indeed, are Persian in every respect. They have an influential colony at Cabul, and are accounted the best-instructed part of the population.

The Hazarah, according to some, are Mongols, introduced by Jengis Khan; according to others, Turkish Usbeks of the Berlas tribe, formerly nomadising near Shazhrisab. Timur in the year 799 of the Hijra despatched a thousand families of this tribe to the valley of Badgis, on the Upper Murghab, where they were called Hazarah, or "Thousanders." Thence they extended as far as Cabul on the east, and Herat on the west. Their division into tribes and clans is very complex, and they are most of them nomads and independent. The Eastern sections of the race owe allegiance to Cabul. Their clans have separate Khans, and are in perpetual feud with each other.

The Usbeks, of the Kutagan tribe, are the descendants of the Turkoman conquerors of Afghanistan, and the ruling element in the Khanates north of the Hindu Kush.

The Hindus belong to the Kshatra or warrior caste, are 300,000 strong, and live chiefly in the towns.

The Jat, also about 300,000 strong, of unknown origin, are probably aborigines. They are scattered over the whole country.

The Kafirs, or Siyahposh, about 150,000, live on the slopes of the Hindu Kush, north of Cabul. Of Caucasian type, their origin remains to be explained. They are divided into eighteen clans. The Swat, Chitrals, and Safi belonging to the aboriginals border upon the Kafirs. They are said to number no less than 500,000 souls.

The Arabs, known as Syads, or descendants of the Prophet, form a compact mass in the district of Kunar, in Northern Cabulistan. They are also found dispersed over the other districts, like Armenians and Jews.

The Afghan tribes frequently intermingle, and increase or decrease in consequence of families leaving their old associations to form new ties. Wars and feuds frequently result in the forcible transfer of tribes, or parts of tribes, to new localities, when embodiment with other tribes usually ensues. The tribes are least distinct in the towns. In some of them only one-fifth of the population are Afghans, four-fifths consisting of Tajiks, Hindus, Jews, Persians, &c.

People, Language, and Antiquities. 77

The most densely-inhabited parts of the country are the valleys of the Cabul and Kuram, with their tributaries. In the wastes that occupy a considerable portion of the southern provinces, people crowd round the rivers, leaving the rest of the country empty. The regions bordering on Baluchistan are the least inhabited. The inhabitants live mostly in villages, isolated tenements being rendered impossible by the frequent wars. The villages, always large and surrounded by walls, frequently—especially in Northern Cabul—have up to 3,000 houses.

The inhabitants are almost exclusively Sunnis, the Hazarah and Kazlbashi alone being Shiahs. The small number of Armenians in the country profess Christianity.

The Kafirs follow a nondescript religion, having some affinity to Hinduism, but none whatever, as some have supposed, to Christianity. Their proper name is Siyahposh (the "black-legged," from their wearing leggings of goat-skins), and they are mentioned by Strabo under the name of Σι Βαξ. Ethnologically they are a most interesting race, having a considerable resemblance to Europeans, and some have supposed them to represent the original Aryan inhabitants of Afghanistan and the regions of the Hindu Kush. The Kafir women are said to be as beautiful as the men are handsome; but before a young man is allowed to marry he is required to furnish proof of having slain a Mussulman.

The Kafirs, however, seem well disposed to the English, and a recent writer says: "The Kafirs look to us as kinsmen and natural allies; but the mountainous tracts of Buner, Swat, and Bajour forbid intercourse, and in the far valleys of Kashgar and of the Kunar river there yet rages the blood feud caused by past wrongs inflicted and received between the idolatrous Kafir and the fanatical Mussulman."

Sir John Kaye has left an eloquent description of the Afghans as they were at the beginning of the century, and they have probably altered very little in character since that time. " The people," he tells us, " were a race—or a group of races—of hardy, vigorous mountaineers. The physical character of the country had stamped itself on the moral conformation of its inhabitants. Brave, independent, but of a turbulent, vindictive character, their very existence seemed to depend upon a constant succession of internal feuds. The wisest of them would probably have shaken their heads in negation of the adage—' Happy is the country whose annals are a blank.' They knew no happiness in anything but strife. It was their delight to live in a state of chronic warfare." It has been said that every Afghan is more or less a soldier or a bandit. The very shepherds carry their matchlocks ready for an affray or a robbery at any moment. It may seem strange that pastoral and predatory habits could thus be blended : but, so it is, "the tented cantonments of the sheep-drivers often bristle into camps of war."

It is but fair to say there is a brighter side to the picture. Outwardly grave, they are of a cheerful, lively disposition, and this, notwithstanding their long beards and sober garments. They are fond of children, and delight in listening to the longest stories, however improbable or romantic. Their generosity and hospitality have been often described. They will entertain strangers without grudging, and their deadliest enemy is secure if he comes beneath their roof. The simplicity of their courtesy is refreshing when contrasted with the polished insincerity of the Persian, or the fierce arrogance of the Indian Pathan. Their respect for truth and honesty would not be great if judged by a Christian standard, but is striking as compared with some of their Asiatic neighbours. They treat their dependents with kindness and consideration, and are rewarded by fidelity and zeal in service. There is little of the tyranny seen in other Eastern countries towards the inmates of the Zanana and domestic slaves. They care less for learning than for manly exercises, and simplicity takes with them the place of wit and eloquence.

Summing up his description of Afghan politics in the time of Zemaun Shah (1800), Sir John Kaye says—"The history of the Afghan monarchy is a history of a long series of revolutions. Seldom has the country rested from strife; seldom has the sword reposed in the scabbard. The temper of the people has never been attuned to peace. They are impatient of the restraints of a settled government, and are continually panting after change. Half a century of turbulence and anarchy has witnessed but little variation in the national character, and the Afghan of the present day is the same strange mixture of impetuosity and cunning, of boldness and treachery, of generosity and selfishness, of kindness and cruelty, as he was when Zemaun Shah haunted the Council Chamber of Calcutta with a phantom of invasion; and the vision was all the more terrible because 'the shape thereof' no one could discern."

The vernacular of a large part of the non-Afghan population is Persian, and this is familiar to all educated Afghans. But the proper language of the Afghans is *Pushtu* or *Pukhtu*, an Aryan or Indo-Persian (not Semitic) dialect. The oldest known work in Pushtu is a "History of the Conquest of Swat," by Shaikh Mali, chief of the Yuzufzais, and leader in the conquest (A.D. 1413-24). Their literature is rich in poetry, Abdurrahman (seventeenth century) being the best known poet.

Major Raverty has made us acquainted with some specimens of Afghan poetry, which convey the idea of deep feeling. Most of it is of the mystical kind so familiar in Persian literature, by which spiritual meaning is hidden in very worldly similes. In the hills to the north, among the Kafirs and other independent and semi-independent tribes, dialects more approaching the Sanskrit type are found.

The judicial institutions of the Afghans are rude in the extreme. The functions of judges in criminal cases are discharged by the popular assemblies of the tribes, assisted by Mullahs or Muhammadan priests. Minor offences are punished by the village elders. The Muhammadan law has of course general authority, but there is a special code of peculiar Afghan usages, known as Pushtun-Wali, which has the force of law. In towns we find the courts of the Muhammadan judges called *Kazis*, aided by the Muftis. The Amir-i-Mahkama is a kind of chief clerk and treasurer, and the Darogha superintends the whole proceedings. Justice, however, is a commodity to be bought very largely here, as in other Muhammadan countries.

We have heard a good deal lately of the large

standing army of Shere Ali, the present Amir. According to some authorities, he has 60,000 men in the field. This is not improbable, seeing that it was believed that Zaman Shah, at the beginning of the century, could collect 200,000 men round his standard for any national object. Of the constitution of the Afghan army our information is necessarily imperfect, but a part of it, at any rate, is modelled on the European system, as far as drill, dress, and equipments are concerned.

Of their arms we have good reason to know something, as the best of them are probably the rifles, Enfield and Snider, supplied to the Amir by former Viceroys of India, to the number of 20,000, with ammunition, as well as a field-battery of guns. The chief difficulty the Afghans have had in using European weapons has been, it is said, from their inability to manufacture percussion-caps for them, and their importation through British India has been prevented by the Indian Government. Native arms are the formidable "jazail," or long-rifled matchlock, with which an Afghan can hit a mark at 800 yards, the sword or knife, and shield.

The following more detailed account of the military strength of Afghanistan, extracted from the records of the Russian Central Staff Office at St. Petersburg, was supplied to the *Times* by its Berlin correspondent in October, and seems to deserve quoting at length :—

"Afghanistan is portioned out among many semi-independent tribes, each of which has a separate ruler and a standing army.

"Cabul and Candahar have a considerable regular force, consisting of infantry, cavalry, and artillery. The greater part of these troops is distributed over rural garrisons, and under the control of the local governors. The regular Cabul force, which does not seem to have been increased in the thirty years intervening between 1838 and 1868, is as follows :— Infantry (Jazailchi), 2,500 men; regular cavalry, 3,000; irregular cavalry, 10,000; artillery, 45 guns. Besides these, there were, in times of peace, one regiment of infantry at Candahar, one regiment at Ghuznee, one regiment and five guns at Kala-i-Ghilzai, one regiment of infantry, one of rifles, and five guns at Kuram, and a force of full 10,000 men, with three batteries, at Balkh. The regular troops are maintained and reinforced by conscription, irregulars being called in as time and circumstances require. In Cabul, the troops receive pay and provisions, a practice which can hardly be said to obtain with any degree of regularity in the provinces. The infantry are armed partly with matchlocks, partly with excellent modern rifles, the gift of the British Government. They also carry swords and daggers.

The Jazailchis, or rifles, are armed with long solid muskets, rested on a forked support when firing, while the cavalry boast a large variety of weapons. The infantry are, many of them, arrayed in cast-off English uniforms, bought up by special agents of the Cabul Government at Peshawar and Sindh. Some regiments wear uniforms of European cut, made of Afghan cloth—the coats are brown, the trousers white. The troops quartered in country towns generally live upon the people. All the Afghan troops endeavour to imitate the Anglo-Indian forces in their tactics, drill, and commissariat service; but in this respect the success of the Cabul military is small in comparison with that of the Herat men.

" The Herat regular force was originally organised by Sultan Jan, and consists of five regiments of infantry of 500 men each, five detachments of cavalry, one in each district, of 450 men each, and eight guns. The whole forms a total of about 5,000. Young men of the peasant class are liable to conscription at an age when they may almost be regarded as children. The cavalry being the more national force, its recruits are supplied by the district authorities. There is a Commander-in-Chief, subject to the personal commands of the Sovereign. The artillery is under the direction of a special commander, the Topchi Bashi. The regiments are divided into companies. Officers' titles are taken from the English army; the Jarnal, Koronel, and Midjar answering respectively to the General, Colonel, and Major. The Sovereign has a special adjutant called Adjutant Bashi, a post occupied in the days of Sultan Jan by a Russian ensign, Prince Vatchnadse. Discipline is exceedingly strict. Commanders have unlimited power, and may kill subordinates with impunity. The soldiers live in special houses with their families, and receive pay, food, uniforms, and arms from the Government. The cavalry, too, get pay from the Government, but have to find their own arms and horses. The infantry are provided with flintlocks, modern rifles, the crooked Afghan sword and daggers, from 1 ft. to 1½ ft. long. The uniform is of light sky-blue cotton, after the English pattern, with ample folds, stand-up collar, and metal buttons. The trousers are of white cotton, very tight and short. They wear a sort of slipper on their naked feet, black Persian hats when on duty, and red flat hats in undress. In the case of recruits these hats are yellow. All the different regiments wear the same uniform. The cavalry are distinguished by the national Afghan dress, and armed with pikes, matchlocks, daggers, and crooked swords. Drill, as a rule, is entrusted to Anglo-Indian deserters, and carried on in accordance with English rules. There is a great deal of regimental service going on, with a fair degree of success in tactics and manœuvring capacity. The word of command is given in English.

"The small Usbek Khanates in Northern Cabulistan also have standing armies, the strength of which some time ago may be seen from the following list :—

	Infantry. Men.	Cavalry. Horses.	Artillery. Guns.
Maimana	100	1,500	—
Shibrgan	1,500	2,000	—
Aktcha	—	200	—
Balkh	10,000	2,500	—
Khulm	—	—	10
Kunduz	—	—	6
Cabulistan—			
Navasai	500	200	—
Lendai Sind	—	—	13
Dyar	400	50	—
Babusi	500	200	—

All these troops are liable to take the field at the summons of the Amir of Cabul, their feudal lord and sovereign. In addition to these regulars there is a militia—a numerous force in a country, every male inhabitant of which is ready to take up arms at a moment's notice. As was proved in 1839, one-eighth of the entire population may be assembled, fully equipped, and sent out with the utmost despatch. By the side of the general levy there is a special militia, called Defteri, whose members have their names registered in time of peace, and are in receipt of a small salary, or a certain quantity of corn, or else enjoy the free use of canal water. The strength and division of the militia is the subject of the following table:—

	Horse.	Infantry.
Cabul	21,000	10,000
Candahar	12,000	6,000
Herat	8,000	10,000
Lash (Siestan)	500	5,000
Khulm	8,000	3,000
Balkh	2,500	1,000
Sir-i-pul	2,000	2,000
Kunduz	2,000	—
Aktcha	200	—
Andhkui	1,800	600
Shibrgan	2,000	500
Maimana	1,500	1,000
Gesaraiz—		
Seidnat	4,000	—
Pusht Kug	5,000	3,000
Yekikholin	1,000	300
Desansji	400	1,200
Sur Jingeli	500	800
Firuz Kugi	3,750	6,400
Kiptchak	—	400
Taimun	1,200	10,000
Total	77,350	61,200

138,550

"Almost every town and village in Afghanistan is surrounded by a brick wall, and may be easily converted into a defensive position. There is also a large number of small towers distributed over the country, for the protection of passes, ravines, and village grounds. Some of these towers, thanks to their advantageous situation, are formidable enough to check the march of European troops, though none could hold out against a regular siege.

"The most important fortress in the western parts is Herat, enclosed within a square wall, each side 4,200 feet in length. The wall is of brick, thirty-five feet high, and stands on ground artificially raised. It is protected by a moat, and on two sides by a glacis, constructed by the English in 1838. Six gates, defended by brick towers, lead to the city. There is also a citadel, Chagar Bagh, in the southeastern corner of the city, likewise built of brick. The town is provided with water by the Hari-rud river. Farrah, another fortress near the Persian frontier, is built on the same plan as Herat, but only half the size. The walls of this place are of a very solid sort of brick. Farrah protects the road from southern Persia to Afghanistan.

"Northern Afghanistan is defended by the fort of Maimana, situated on a small river, in a mountainous region. Its wall is five feet thick and 12 feet high. The moat is shallow.

"On the eastern frontier there is Jalalabad, a place of respectable strength, but now abandoned. The citadel of Cabul is likewise a strong place, and accessible only by a winding path. The citadel can hold out against a prolonged siege, and commands the town, which has no walls.

"In the interior of Afghanistan the most important fort is Ghazni, the citadel of which was accounted unconquerable before its capture by the English. Candahar is a large but weak fortress, being commanded by adjacent heights. The place has no glacis and an insignificant moat. It is easy to cut off the water supply. The citadel occupies the northern part of the town.

"All the important roads of Afghanistan lead from east to west, and are merely tracks, without the slightest attempt at assisting nature. In the more open parts, however, they are serviceable for vehicles and field artillery. Taking Herat as a starting point, we have a whole network of roads leading respectively to Mash-had, Merv, Maimana, Candahar, and Siestan."

ANTIQUITIES.

Under this head we have only room for a brief notice of two or three of the more celebrated "relics of the past."

The first of these are the caves of Bamian. Up to the present day we have no complete description of them, nor, as far as we know, any careful drawings of the objects; but when they have been properly described and photographed these remains at Bamian will probably rank as wonders in celebrity with the Rock-cut Temples of India, or the Pyramids of Egypt. There are some slight accounts of the place in more than one writer, from which we may gather some idea of the archæological remains at this spot. It is about eighty miles in a straight line to the north-west of Cabul, and is on the direct road between that town and Balkh, and in one of the principal passes leading to the valley of the Oxus. The high road from Bactria to India went through this Pass, and it was on the line of conquest in the time of Alexander. In the Pass there is a high cliff of rock, extending for some distance, and the whole face of the rock is perforated with a multitude of caves. These are all excavated, and have galleries of communication and stairs, also excavated, so that the rock resembles a piece of sponge, and have been compared with the City of Caverns at Inkermann. In addition to the caves there are two niches hollowed out in the face of the scarp, and in these niches the rock has been carved into two enormous figures about 100 feet high. There is a third and smaller figure which has no niche; some projecting mass of rock has been cut away, and the figure left standing out into the valley. As we have no exact date to go upon, it cannot be said as yet whether these figures existed or not when Alexander with his Macedonian hosts went past. Certainly these figures must have looked down on many conquerors as they went on towards the Indus. In our own period a battle was fought in the valley under these figures, between Dost Muhammad and Brigadier Dennie, on the 18th September, 1840. Later still another battle took place between the sons of Dost Muhammad, when they were fighting for the throne after his death.

The Greeks who went with Alexander reported that they had seen the Cave of Prometheus in the Paropamisus, or the Indian Caucasus, and some writers conclude, as the geographical position suits the theory, that this report must have been founded on the caves at Bamian, and that they existed at that time. The Hindoos ascribe them to the "Panch Pandu Ke Bhai," or the Five Pandu Brothers, who are something like the Cyclops of the Greeks or giants of the Northern nations, and get the credit of all gigantic works. There is a long ridge of rock like a petrified serpent, the origin of which is thus described :—According to the Hindu legend, Arjuna, one of the five brothers, went out walking, and when about four miles away he found on his path a snake of huge dimensions and of dreadful shape. It attempted to swallow up Arjuna, but he struck it dead at the first blow, cutting it into two halves. The stony monster is still to be seen, and still resembles a serpent, with water flowing through it. This is, no doubt, some old aqueduct connected with the water supply of the place, to which the story has been tacked on. The Muhammadans call the two principal figures Lat and Manat, and identify them with two idols, which have similar names, mentioned in the fifty-third chapter of the Koran.

These are only a few of the traditions which, as might be expected, such a very remarkable place as this has given birth to. The general impression is that the ruins belong to the Buddhist period. According to this theory, the caves were the cells of a vast monastery of Buddhist monks. At Ajunta, near Bombay, as well as at other places, there are numerous caves of this description. Such places are called Viharas, and every monk had his separate cell; while some of the larger caves were called Chaityas, and in them they met as a congregation for worship. From one or two slight sketches of the colossal figures which have been brought home, it is thought that a resemblance can be traced to the style of the Buddhist figures found in the Peshawar district, which seems to bear evidence of Greek influence. If this theory of these caves and figures being Buddhist should turn out to be the true one, then, as Buddhism is not supposed to have progressed so far north at the date of Alexander's march upon India, the conclusion will be that they did not exist at his time. Religious ascetics who lived in the woods and in caves most probably existed long before Buddhism, and it is quite possible that there may have been caves at Bamian at a very early period, and they might have originated the story of the Cave of Prometheus. If we suppose that the place had acquired a celebrity for holy men, it would be exactly such a place which the Buddhist monks would adopt for their Viharas; and, if they did this, they may have extended the caves and produced the large figures, which, so far as we can at present judge, seem to be figures of Buddha. A few accurate plans of the caves and a careful sketch or two of the figures would soon put this point beyond dispute.

The following relic belongs to a later period of Afghan history. The tomb of Mahmud still exists, and the two celebrated minars of red brick are still erect, but the mosques to which they belonged have long since passed away.

The "Gates of Somnath" were supposed to have been removed by Mahmud of Ghazni, along with the other treasure of the temple, which he plundered in the course of his last invasion of India. These gates were of sandalwood, and were said to have been placed on his tomb. This piece of history, although dating as far back as the end of the tenth century, was so well known over India that on our troops having retrieved the reputation which was supposed to have been lost in the Cabul disasters, the gates on Mahmud's tomb were brought back by the conquering army, and Lord Ellenborough's proclamation pointed out to the Hindoos that these gates of their temple, which had been carried off as trophies by Mahmud, we had again borne back as trophies, and as visible evidence to the people of India that our arms had triumphed, and that our power was supreme. So celebrated was this event at the time that Lord Ellenborough was represented in caricatures as a new Samson carrying off the gates of Gaza. The military authorities who brought these relics away had assumed that the wooden gates on the tomb of Mahmud must necessarily be the sandalwood gates of Somnath, but if they had had only a very slight knowledge of Indian art, these gates would most probably never have been heard of. It was only when the political fuss was ended and the gates were resting in peace, that those who knew something of Indian ornament began to inspect them, and declared, in spite even of the Governor-General's proclamation, that they could not possibly be the gates of Somnath. Those who neither knew nor cared for art refused to accept this judgment, but a microscope demonstrated that the wood of which they were made was deodar pine, and not sandalwood. That they are not the gates of the old Hindu shrine is now an accepted point. If the sandalwood gates ever really went to Ghazni and ornamented the tomb of Mahmud, they must have been destroyed at some time or other, and new ones had been made of deodar, a wood which grows plentifully on the Safed Koh and the Hindu Kush. The ornament upon them is so distinctly Muhammadan that the wonder is no one with the avenging army was able to discern the truth and point out the inevitable conclusion.

CHAPTER IV.

ALEXANDER THE GREAT'S MARCH THROUGH AFGHANISTAN ON INDIA.

Alexander's Army—Pursuit of Darius After the Battle of Arbela—Conquest of Parthia and Hyrcania—Founding of Herat—Conquest of North-Eastern Afghanistan—Campaign in Bactria—Alexander an Oriental Potentate—Marriage with Roxana—Crosses the Hindu Kush into India—Campaign in India—Voyage of Nearchus from the Indus to the Euphrates—Alexander's March Across the Desert of Baluchistan —Greek Influence on the Oxus.

THE first invasion of India from the West in historical times deserves more than a passing notice, as exhibiting the vast difference in the conditions of conquest which the inventions of modern times have imported into the art of war. From the day when Alexander, son of Philip, a youth not yet twenty-two years of age, but generalissimo of the armies of Greece, marched from Pella in Macedonia to the conquest of Asia, his small, but highly disciplined army received no check in its steady course of victory, till its own mutinous refusal to go further made the great conqueror turn back from the banks of the Satlaj. The army with which Alexander set out, in April 334 B.C., numbered 30,000 infantry and 4,500 cavalry. The historian tells us that the smallness of this force must not be viewed as a matter of vague wonder, seeing that one of the three modes by which an invader may attempt the conquest of a country is by "the movable column, which throws itself into the heart of an enemy's country, trusting to rapid success for safety."

When we remember what this "movable column" did, how for eleven years it marched over the greater part of Asia west of the Indus—reinforced, it is true, by fresh levies from Macedon, and absorbing into its ranks many of the Greek mercenaries that were found in Asia Minor—how, besides fighting great battles against incalculable odds, it traversed trackless deserts, crossed lofty mountains and mighty rivers, and, moreover, founded cities which remain to this day, it may be safely remarked that it did what no movable column ever did before, has done since, or is likely to do to the end of the world's history.

The countries through which this army passed from Macedonia to Babylon were, doubtless, not unwilling to see in the youthful conqueror a deliverer from the hated Persian yoke, and the terrible examples which he set at Tyre and Gaza may have had much to do with "securing his rear." The moral effect of the battles of the Granicus and of the Issus was enormous, so that distant cities sent to announce their submission.

It is, however, with Alexander's most wonderful marches that we have to do now, which he made after the Battle of Arbela, in pursuit of the Persian Monarch, whose last hope was thus broken ; and afterwards in the conquest of his most outlying provinces, those of Aria (*Herat*), Drangiana (*Seistan*), Arachosia (*Candahar*), Bactria (*Balkh*), Sogdiana (*Samarcand*), to the confines of Scythia, beyond the Jaxartes (*Syr Darya*), on the north, and of the Gandaridæ, beyond the Hyphasis (*Satlaj*) on the east. After the conqueror had come up with the fugitive King, Darius, only to find him dead in his chariot, transfixed by the spears of his satraps, who wished to deprive the victorious invader of any advantage he might have derived from the possession of the Monarch's person as a prisoner, Alexander rejoined his main army, and set before it the task of subjugating the northern and eastern provinces, beginning with Parthia and Hyrcania, to the east of the Caspian. Thence he quickly passed into Aria, and here he founded the city of Alexandria Ariorum, the modern *Herat*. Reserving Bactria for his last attack, he turned southwards into Drangiana (*Seistan*), on the banks of the river Erymandus (*Helmand*). His stay at the capital Prophthasia was rendered but too memorable by the fate of Philotas and his father Parmenio, whose death for alleged treason followed upon the reports of some self-laudatory speeches displeasing to their master which they were said to have made.

Having spent the winter in completing the conquest of the provinces which occupy the north-eastern part of the table-land of what is now Afghanistan—during which time he founded two more cities, Alexandria in Arachosia (probably *Candahar*), and Alexandria ad Caucasum, about fifty miles north-west of Cabul—he crossed the Hindu Kush, while the passes were still covered with snow. His soldiers, whose imagination had been fed with the traditions of the Greek poets respecting Mount Caucasus, to pass which they deemed the highest achievement of foreign adventure, either conceived this range to be a continuation of that chain, or flattered their chief into the belief that it was so by applying to it the title of the "Indian Caucasus."

Alexander was now in Bactria, having crossed, in all probability, by the Bamian, the only one of the four principal passes over the Hindu Kush practicable in winter. Bessus, the last of the satraps to yield, had crossed from Bactria, his own province, which he was too weak to defend, into Sogdiana, on the other side of the Oxus (*Amu*). Alexander pressed on through the sandy deserts, amidst great sufferings, to the most difficult river he had yet crossed, and transported his army on their tent-skins, filled with air and straw—a mode of transport which is represented on the old Assyrian sculptures. After the capture of Bessus and his punishment for the murder of Darius had been decreed, Alexander gave a proof of the growth of Oriental vices in his character by the massacre of the Greek colony of the Branchidæ, in Sogdiana—the descendants of the guardians of the temple of Apollo, near Miletus, who had surrendered its treasures to Xerxes, by whom they were removed to Sogdiana, out of reach of the vengeance of the Greeks. Having taken Maracanda (*Samarcand*), the capital of Sogdiana, Alexander advanced to the Jaxartes (*Syr Darya*).

On its banks he founded the most distant of the cities that bore his name, Alexandreschata (probably on the site of *Khojend*), near that which marked the limits of the Empire of Cyrus, who had failed in that attempt to subdue the Scythians, which Alexander proposed soon to renew.

Returning for the winter (B.C. 339) to Bactria, or Zariaspé (the modern *Balkh*), he was recalled to Sogdiana in the following year, to put down a formidable revolt headed by the late Satrap Spitamenes. It was after this successful campaign and on his return to Maracanda, that the fatal banquet was held at which the great conqueror, in a fit of drunken passion, slew his bosom friend, Clitus. The only relief which he could find from the pangs of remorse at this act was in renewed action. For a whole year the Sogdians, assisted by the Scythians, carried on a desultory warfare with Alexander's invincible army, during which it penetrated their deserts and mountains, and subdued their fortresses, until Spitamenes was slain by his Sogdian allies, and his head sent to Alexander. It was at the famous storming of the impregnable "Sogdian rock" that the beautiful Roxana, the daughter of a Bactrian chief, who afterwards became the first Asiatic wife of Alexander, fell into his hands as a captive. The marriage was celebrated with great pomp at Bactria, and Alexander showed his progress towards Orientalism by attempting to exact the ceremony of prostration even from his Greek followers.

With the return of summer Alexander left Bactria to re-cross the Paropamisus (*Koh-i-baba*) and subdue the still unknown lands of India. That name appears but once or twice in ancient history; as a region that excited, only to disappoint, the ambition of conquerors such as Semiramis, Darius, and Alexander; and chiefly known, after his time, by the rich products by which it rewarded the commercial enterprise which had its centre at Alexandria. The India with which Alexander made his brief acquaintance of a year or two, was only the region so-called in the proper, but narrower, sense of the name, the *Land of the Indus* and its tributaries; in other words, *Sindh* and the *Panjab*, or country of the *Five Rivers*. The details of Alexander's march through Afghanistan are full of interest for the geographer, but are chiefly remarkable for the historian, on account of the facility with which he subdued the mountaineers, whose descendants have proved so troublesome in our time. The campaign, like his former passage of the Paropamisus, was made in the depth of winter. Following the course of the river Cophen (*Cabul*), he crossed the Indus near Attock, and was met by the prince of the country that lay between the Indus and the Hydaspes (*Jhilam*), who came out to meet Alexander with valuable presents, amongst which were twenty-five war-elephants, and brought a reinforcement of 5,000 men. We would gladly linger over the recital of Alexander's battle with Porus (said to be a corruption of the Sanscrit *Paurusha*, a hero, and, therefore, rather a title than a name of an individual), which was fought on the left bank of the Hydaspes (*Jhilam*). The Indian King became a tributary to the conqueror, who founded the town of Nicœa, to commemorate the victory. The rest of the Panjab was easily subdued. The swollen stream of the Acesines (*Chenab*) was crossed on inflated skins; and the Hydrastes *(Ravi)* with less difficulty. The

Cathœans and other independent tribes made some resistance, but their capital, Sangala (probably *Lahore*), was stormed ; 17,000 of the inhabitants being put to the sword, and 70,000 taken prisoners.

Alexander had now reached the farthest limits of his conquests. At the Hyphasis (*Satlaj*) his ambition was stirred afresh by the intelligence that he could in eleven days be on the great Ganges River, and meet in battle the powerful nation of the Gandaridæ. But the soldiers of his army, even the officers, who might have been supposed to share his longing for universal conquest, refused to proceed further, and Alexander wept, " not that there were no regions left to conquer, but because he was at length made to feel the curb which dependence on fellow-men imposes on the strongest will."

His return was marked by the same daring spirit that had characterised his advance. Instead of retracing his steps through what is now called the Khaibar Pass, he adopted the plan of following the course of the Indus to its mouth, and exploring the shores of the Indian Ocean to the Euphrates. Before leaving the Hyphasis twelve immense altars were built on its banks to mark the furthest limits of his progress, in imitation of Hercules and Dionysus. At the Hydaspes he was joined by a reinforcement which had marched from Europe, a fact which testifies to the wonderful tranquillity of his Empire. It should not be forgotten, too, that Alexander's double march across the Panjab was performed during the rainy season.

It is difficult in these days to estimate the magnitude of the daring involved in that wonderful voyage, on which Nearchus, Alexander's Admiral, now embarked. Nine months were occupied in reaching the mouth of the Indus. The difficulty of the voyage was enhanced by the barrenness of the shores along which it lay, for navigation then was dependent on communication with the land. He brought the fleet safely, however, to the port of Harmozia (*Ormuz*), where he landed to report progress to Alexander in Carmania, and then returned to complete the voyage to the Euphrates. He finally rejoined Alexander on the Pasitigris, near Susa, about February, B.C. 325, having set sail from the Indus at the preceding autumnal equinox. His reward of a crown of gold was merited.

Meanwhile, Alexander with his veterans had been accomplishing his celebrated march through the deserts of Gedrosia (*Baluchistan*), in which he shared to the full the terrible sufferings of fatigue and thirst with his soldiers. The remainder of the march was through his recently-conquered Persian provinces, and appears to have been free from difficulty.

Although the outlying provinces of Alexander's empire fell away in rapid succession after his death—

Bactria alone remaining a Greek kingdom as late as B.C. 125, when it was overthrown by the Parthians, who had previously shorn the empire of all the other provinces beyond the Euphrates—a distinct Hellenising influence pervaded these new Asiatic kingdoms from the large intermixture of Greek elements in their government, their population, and their language. It would be beyond the limits assigned to this work to enter further into this interesting subject, but the materials are available for its pursuit, and few fields of research are more inviting. The visible material monuments of Greek influence which are known to exist in these regions, and those which still await discovery, may yet throw much light upon the early history of the present races that occupy the countries round the Oxus and the valleys of the Hindu Kush and its connected chains.

CHAPTER V.

AFGHAN HISTORY FROM MUHAMMAD TO ZAMAN SHAH.

First Appearance of Afghanistan in Mediæval History—Arab Settlements—Story of Kasim and the Rajpût Princess—The Ghazni Monarchy Founded by Alptagin— Invasion of India— Peshawar the First Permanent Muhammadan Conquest in India—Sabaktagin—Plunder of Somnath—Mahmud of Ghazni—Shahabuddin—Jengis Khan—Timur or Tamerlane Invades Northern India—Babar Founds the Mughal Empire of India—Nadir Shah Invades and Plunders the Panjab—Ahmad Shah Founds the Durani Empire of Afghanistan—Invades India—Battle of Panipat—Zaman Shah—Threatens to Invade India.

WE may date the appearance of Afghanistan in mediæval history from the forty-third year after the Hijra,* or flight of Muhammad from Mecca to Medina. The warriors of Islam, urged on by fanatical zeal on the one hand, and love of plunder on the other, had quickly overrun Central Asia, and in A.D. 664 had advanced to Cabul, while the intervening provinces of Persia had been already brought under the sway of the Arab Caliphs. We need not attempt to trace the fluctuations of power that followed the first Arab settlements in Afghanistan.

* A.D. 622.

Suffice it to say that they resulted in the acceptance of the Muhammadan faith, and a nominal, if not in some instances an actual, submission to the central Muhammadan government. The further extension of Muhammadan power into Northern India did not succeed beyond a temporary hold on Sindh by Kasim early in the eighth century. This Kasim was nephew of Hejaz, Governor of Basra (*Bassorah*) and it is he of whom the story is related which the lovers of Eastern romance never tire of telling. Two beautiful daughters of the Rajah Dahu having fallen into his hands, Kasim despatched them as a present to the Caliph's harem. Arrived at Damascus, one of them, who had attracted the Caliph's gaze, declared herself unworthy of his attention, owing to her having been dishonoured by Kasim. In obedience to the royal mandate Kasim was executed in Sindh, and his body sewn up in a raw hide and sent to the Caliph. When the body arrived at Damascus the Princess admitted her falsehood, but gloried in having thus avenged her father's death. It may be doubted whether this legend is strictly true; but it is certain that, by Kasim's death or recall, the Muhammadan power in Sindh was much weakened, and, after a time, became a mere tradition. Caliph Haroun-al-Raschid (to adopt the traditional orthography) died in A.D. 806, and the Arab Caliphate was not long in dissolving.

Khorasan and Trans-Oxiana became independent under the Tahirites, or successors of Tahir, who had successfully headed a rebellion.

To them succeeded the Sofarides, in A.D. 872; the founder of this short-lived dynasty being Yakub, a brazier of Seistan. These gave way to the Samanis, in A.D. 903, a dynasty which continued to exist in Central Asia for 120 years.

The fifth prince, Abdul-Malik, possessed a Turki slave named Alptagin, to whom he had committed the high office of governor of Khorasan. In A.D. 961 he had to flee from the suspicious anger of his patron's successor on the throne, and having escaped with a few followers to Ghazni, an outlying province to the south-eastward, flanked by the Suliman Mountains, he made himself independent, by the aid chiefly of the rude Afghan population of that region.

We have alluded elsewhere to the claim which Afghan chroniclers have set up to a Jewish descent. Apart from this tradition, the earliest account we have of the Afghans is their establishment in the east of the table-land, where they were found efficient allies by Alptagin. The son of Alptagin, who succeeded to the newly-erected throne of Ghazni on his father's death in A.D. 976, died (according to Farishta, the Persian historian) in less than two years without issue, and Sabaktagin, who, like Alptagin, had been a slave, but had risen to such favour as to be admitted to an alliance with the daughter of Alptagin, was elected to succeed the latter's son.

Sabaktagin, although bought by a merchant in Turkestan as a slave, claimed descent from Yazdagird, the last of the Persian kings. His talent in warlike enterprise, chiefly against the Indian tribes on the Indus, had commended him to notice, and gained him the throne.

He was not long in subduing Candahar, which he annexed to his small kingdom of Ghazni, and then set his face towards India. He invaded the Panjab, took forts, built mosques, and carried off a large booty, thereby setting the example which other invaders of India never failed to imitate.

This was not suffered to pass without an attempt at revenge, and we soon find an immense army— the best of the Aryan chivalry—led by the Kings of Lahore, Delhi, Ajmir, Kalinga, and Kananj, assembled to resist the aggressive Ghaznavites. Twice did a great Hindu army march across the Indus. The first time a furious storm so disheartened the superstitious Hindus that they sued for terms instead of giving battle. On the second occasion the Muhammadans were victorious, and took possession of the Valley of Peshawar, their first permanent occupation of Indian territory.

Sabaktagin did not renew his attacks on India,

and died in A.D. 997. His illegitimate son, Mahmud of Ghazni, first defeated his legitimate brother, Ismail, who had been nominated successor, and then obtained the whole kingdom, which he enlarged to a greater extent than had been done by Sabaktagin. During his reign of thirty-three years, he made ten great invasions of India, the last being directed against the sacred temple of Somnath, to destroy which seemed an act of great virtue to the zealous Muhammadan Sultan, for he had assumed this title. The Brahmins offered an immense sum if he would spare the sacred temple, but he replied that he wished to be known to posterity as "Mahmud the Idol-breaker," and not as the "Idol-seller." He himself struck off the nose of the idol, which was nine feet high, and was rewarded for his religious zeal by finding in its inside precious stones and pearls of a value far exceeding what had been offered, and the other wealth of the temple was immense. Invaders in all ages have been rarely afflicted with twinges of conscience in the matter of spoiling the temples and palaces of the countries they honour with their presence. The armies of even such civilised nations as France and England found it impossible to resist the temptation to plunder the royal palaces of Pekin. We are aware that there are always excellent reasons forthcoming to defend such acts in modern times, and we veil the real motive of such deeds—the love of plunder—by alleging the necessity of "reading the barbarians a salutary lesson;" "striking awe into the enemy;" and so on. We do not read that Mahmud of Ghazni troubled himself to make any such hypocritical excuses for his very natural conduct. It is said to his credit, however, that if he plundered temples and murdered priests in the name of religion, he committed no revengeful massacres or wanton executions upon the people generally, or his prisoners. "Tried by the slanders of his times," says the modern historian, "Mahmud must be considered, on the whole, humane, and his unquenchable thirst for plunder is the worst feature of his character." At his death, his dominions extended as far as Ispahan, westward, and a great part of India owned his supremacy. Altogether, he invaded India thirteen times, but ten only of these inroads were of consequence.

Mahmud's dynasty lasted till A.D. 1159, and was succeeded by the house of Ghor, which reigned in Afghanistan till the death of Shahabuddin, in 1206. For the events of this period, which are of the most thrilling interest to the student of early Afghan and Indian history, we must refer the reader to the works of Elphinstone and other historians. We can here take but a very cursory view of the period. After Shahabuddin's death, his successor, Mahmud, resigned India to Kutb-ud-din, originally a slave, but subsequently a great general, to whom the late monarch chiefly owed his conquests in India. In 1215, Tajuddin Elduz, the successor of Mahmud on the throne of Ghazni, attempted to regain his Indian dominions, but failed, and was taken prisoner.

Meanwhile, in A.D. 1217, the first echoes of the name of Jengis Khan, the Mughal conqueror, afterwards so dreaded throughout Western Asia, were heard. He invaded the dominion of the Sultan of Kharizm, overran the country, and penetrated as far as Ghazni. His career of conquest did not, however, extend to India. We cannot attempt to follow in detail the course of Mughal conquest during the next two centuries. In A.D. 1398, Timur or Tamerlane, himself a Tartar, headed the most famous, though by no means the first, Mughal invasion of India, and was proclaimed Emperor of India. He only remained, however, fifteen days in Delhi, and then returned home, after a general and indiscriminate massacre of the people.

From 1478 to 1526, an Afghan dynasty (Lodi) reigned over Northern India, simultaneously with the rule of the Mughals, descendants of Timur, at Cabul, although their capital was at Samarcand. The most celebrated of these last, Babar, sixth in descent from Timur, invaded India in 1526, at the invitation of a member of the Afghan family that ruled at Delhi, and founded the Mughal dynasty of

India. On the death of Babar, Afghanistan, and the whole of the Panjab, became a separate kingdom, under his son Kamran. The history of Afghanistan for the next two centuries is almost inextricably mixed up with that of Persia and Hindostan, the plains of Afghanistan being divided more or less equally between these empires. To those, however, who rejected a foreign yoke the mountains afforded an asylum.

In 1720, the Afghan tribes threw off their allegiance to Persia, and, advancing into the country, took Ispahan. In 1728, they were compelled to retrace their steps by Nadir Shah, the celebrated usurper, who followed up his advantage by occupying the whole of Afghanistan, the western provinces of which were still a nominal dependency of the Delhi kings.

Then followed Nadir Shah's invasion of India, into the causes of which we cannot now enter. Suffice it to say, that the Persian king surpassed former invaders in the booty he obtained, carrying off treasure valued at from £9,000,000 to £30,000,000 sterling, besides the celebrated peacock-throne, which Tavernier valued at £6,000,000, but which other authorities make to have been worth only £2,000,000. The King's share was £15,000,000. On leaving Delhi, Nadir Shah presented Muhammad Shah, the conquered Emperor of India, with his crown, and seated him on his throne; but he annexed to his own dominions all the western provinces of the empire beyond the passes, together with Multan and Sindh.

On the death of Nadir Shah, in 1747, an Afghan officer, of the Durani or Abdali tribe, who had obtained a high command in Nadir Shah's army, united the Afghan tribes into a monarchy under himself. He was young, ambitious, and capable; and, mindful of the rich spoil India had recently furnished, turned his attention to that empire. His invasions were continued till the famous Battle of Panipat, fought on January 7th, 1761, when the Mahratta forces were completely defeated. Ahmad Shah did not assume the government of India, but contented himself with his Afghan kingdom and the Panjab. It may be noted that Clive had broken the power of the Muhammadan ruler of Bengal at the Battle of Plassy, on June 22nd, 1757, three and a-half years before the victory of the Afghan king over the Mahrattas at Panipat. The foundation of the British Empire in India may justly be dated from Clive's famous victory.

Ahmad Shah died in 1773, and was succeeded by an indolent and despotic son, Timur Shah, who left his throne to his two sons, Humayun and Zaman Shah. In the conflict for undivided rule which followed, Zaman Shah was victorious.

In 1798, Zaman Shah wrote to the Governor-General of India, Lord Mornington, announcing his intention of invading Hindostan, and claiming the assistance of the English. At the same time Tippu Sahib, the Sultan of Mysore, was urging Zaman Shah to advance and join him in a crusade against all infidels. Tippu was also in league with the French Government, from whom he looked for assistance against the English. Napoleon had landed in Egypt, and Tippu looked forward to his rapid conquest of that country, and anticipated a triumphant march of the French conqueror across Asia into India, following the precedent of the great "Sekandar," as Alexander the Great is designated in India.

But we have now carried our necessarily brief and imperfect review of Afghan history to the point where Afghan politics come into contact with those of the nations of Western Europe, and it will be convenient to continue the narrative in another chapter.

CHAPTER VI.

AFGHAN HISTORY FROM ZAMAN SHAH TO THE EVE OF THE FIRST AFGHAN WAR.

Zaman Shah Advances to Lahore—Panic in British India—Review of Situation—Native Feeling in India—Incidents of Former Invasions—Alarm at French Intrigues—First Symptoms of "Russophobia"—Encroachment of Russia on Persia—Scheme of Joint Russian and French Invasion of India—Sir John Kaye on the Two Classes of Governor-General—Lords Minto and Wellesley Compared with Lord Lytton—The Rise of the Sikhs—British and Russian Advance Compared—Mission to the Sikhs—Shah Suja—Rise of the Barakzais—Shah Suja an Exile—Affairs in Afghanistan before the First Afghan War—Mission of Captain Burnes and Siege of Herat—Eldred Pottinger—Dost Muhammad—Sikhs Gain Peshawar—Russia Invades Persia—New Russo-Persian Boundary—British Policy.

ZAMAN SHAH, King of the Afghans, the grandson of Ahmad Shah, cherished, as we have said, designs of Indian conquest similar to those that had impelled his grandfather to the invasion of the Panjab. We have seen that in 1798 he had invoked the assistance of the English Governor-General against the Mahrattas, who had established themselves virtually as the most powerful State in Northern India, although the Mughal Emperor at Delhi remained nominally supreme. The Afghan King had advanced as far as

Lahore, with the avowed object of extending the Durani Empire (as it was called after its consolidation by Ahmad Shah) to the Ganges. But he was compelled precipitately to return to resist an invasion of Khorasan by the Persian troops. In the previous year he had been similarly recalled to put down a rebellion headed by his brother Mahmud. For years afterwards the threat of an Afghan invasion kept the British Indian Empire in a chronic state of alarm, and Lord Wellesley, immediately on his accession to the office of Governor-General, had augmented the native army on this account.

However ridiculous now this constant panic may seem to us, it must be remembered that at the beginning of the century the English in India knew little of the resources of the Durani Empire, and less of the people, and their monarch's unfitness for a great enterprise. Nor were the fears entertained so groundless as may appear at first sight. The numerous enemies of the English in India looked to Cabul for deliverance from their encroaching empire with, says Kaye, "malicious expectancy." From the rocky defiles of that romantic country they expected to see swarms of the Faithful hasten to save Islam from the yoke of the usurping Feringhees. All the Muhammadan princes from Tippu in Mysore to Vazir Ali in Oudh, had promised money and men, and even Hindu rajahs had avowed their sympathy with the cause. What Sir John Kaye says of his own day (1857) reads rather strangely now, when we are told that thoughts of an invasion of India again agitate the breasts of some among Shere Ali's advisers. He writes: "We, who in these times trustingly contemplate the settled tranquillity of the north-western provinces of India, and remember Zaman Shah only as the old, blind pensioner of Ludhiana, can hardly estimate aright the real importance of the threatened movement."

If the English in India felt such anxiety at the prospect of an Afghan invasion, how are we to picture to ourselves the feelings of the unprotected myriads who knew by tradition what were the tender mercies they might expect from barbarous hordes such as those that swooped down upon the plains of India with Tamerlane the Tartar, Nadir Shah the Persian, and Ahmad Shah the Durani. The historian tells us that when Tamerlane (or Timur) invaded India, his army pillaged the Panjab up to Delhi, taking vast numbers of captives. Finding it troublesome to carry these along with him, he ordered all of them above the age of fifteen—to the number, says Farishta, of 100,000—to be put to death in cold blood.

The refusal of the people of Delhi to pay a heavy contribution brought upon them a general and indiscriminate massacre and plunder, during

From Zaman Shah to Dost Muhammad. 119

which the monarch gave a great entertainment to his officers.

Again, in 1738, Nadir Shah gave orders at Delhi for a general massacre; and when his soldiers had feasted on blood they gave themselves up for fifty-eight days to plunder, which they sought from the Emperor's palace to the lowest hovels of the poor.

In 1755, Ahmad Shah proceeded to Delhi, and extorted a vast sum of money from the people by torture and massacre. He then attacked the rich city of Mathura, while a religious festival was being held; and thousands of Hindu worshippers were slaughtered without mercy by the Afghans.

After the Battle of Panipat, in 1761, referred to before, between Ahmad Shah and the Mahrattas, which ended in the victory of the Afghans, we read that, "Of all that were taken in the [Indian] camp, women and children became slaves, and next morning the males were cruelly butchered in cold blood."

Such are some of the gentle memories which the barbarians west of the Suliman and Hindu Kush Mountains have left with the people of the plains of Northern India. What wonder that, in 1798, when another attack was threatened from the same quarter, the English, who only echoed the sentiments of their native subjects, should have viewed it with alarm.

It was not, however, simply the Durani King

who was dreaded. The French Emperor was credited with designs of almost universal conquest. The French were known to be eager for an alliance with Persia, and what was more probable to the minds of the rulers of British India then than that an offensive alliance between France, Persia, and Cabul should make those dangers, that once merely seemed to threaten them from the north-west, only too real and imminent.

The great object then appeared to be to gain the friendship of Persia, so that by this means French intrigue might be baffled in Central Asia. In that case, also, Zaman Shah would have in Persia a British ally behind him, ready to avail herself of his absence on the Indian frontier to invade and reclaim some of the provinces of Afghanistan that had once belonged to her. To bring about so favourable a condition of affairs, Lord Wellesley, therefore, sent Captain Malcolm as Envoy of the British Indian Government to Persia.

It is not possible in these pages to trace the history of the negotiations that followed, in which the rare spectacle was seen of an English Ambassador from the Court of St. James, acting in almost open hostility to the British Indian Government. The end to be sought was to keep Persia friendly to ourselves, and prevent French influence gaining any ground.

To understand the politics of that day another Power has to be taken into account, and that Power is Russia. That formidable northern State had been extending its conquests eastwards for years, before the Shah of Persia, in 1805, addressed a letter to Napoleon, whose fortunes were then at their highest point, requesting aid from the Western "Rustam" to stem the tide of Russian aggression. "Before," says Sir John Kaye, "the English trader had begun to organise armies in Hindostan, and to swallow up ancient principalities, the grand idea of founding an Eastern Empire had been grasped by the capacious mind of Peter the Great." The policy he inaugurated was zealously followed by his successors for more than a century. Especially had Russian ambition been directed to acquiring the country between the Black Sea and the Caspian. A small part of it, held by a race of sturdy, brave mountaineers, still declines to bow to the rule of the Czar, and, from time to time, when efforts to subjugate them are made, the natural difficulties of the country to the invaders aids the people in disposing of their assailants. But Georgia had been conquered from the Persians before the beginning of the century, after a succession of wars notorious for their cruel and barbarous incidents. Thus Russia and Persia had, in 1800, become conterminous, and perpetual struggles between the great Russian frontier officers and the Persians marked the early years of the century. Treachery and cruelty mark the annals of this period. The Russian general had received orders to extend the Russian frontier to the river Aras, and nothing short of that boundary would satisfy him. It was when matters seemed at their blackest that the Persian Court applied to Napoleon.

The French emissaries, who soon after found their way to Tehcran, not only persuaded the Persians that England was an effete nation, doomed to fall before Napoleon, and, therefore, not of value as a friend, but negotiations were on foot for a Franco-Persian treaty for the joint invasion of India by a French and Persian army.

It is believed that a treaty to this effect was actually sent home for the approval of Napoleon.

But any hopes Persia may have entertained of French aid against Russia in return for her services against the English in India were doomed to disappointment by the peaceful meeting of the Emperor Alexander and Napoleon Buonaparte upon the river Breinen, near Tilsit, in July, 1807, when a bloody campaign was ended by a scene, in which the two Emperors "embraced like brothers." Among the joint schemes of conquest the two Emperors discussed, one was an invasion of India by a confederate army uniting on the plains of Persia.

Lucien Buonaparte, the brother of Napoleon, was sent to Teheran on a mission to prepare the way for a hostile demonstration against British India in the spring.

The "non-intervention" policy of the English Government was now regarded as out of place. Lord Minto was Governor-General, and felt that action was called for. Sir John Kaye makes a remark concerning this crisis, which we cannot refrain from quoting, as its application at the present juncture of Indian affairs to the supposed rival policies of Lord Lytton and Lord Lawrence, the former an ex-diplomatist, and the latter one who rose from the ranks of the East India Company's service, cannot but be acknowledged.

He says:—" It is observable that statesmen trained in the Cabinets and Courts of Europe have ever been more sensitively alive to the dangers of invasion from the North than those whose experience has been gathered in the fields of Indian diplomacy. Lord Wellesley and Lord Minto were ever tremulous with intense apprehension of danger from without, whilst Sir John Shore and Sir George Barlow possessed themselves in comparative confidence and tranquillity, and if they were not wholly blind to the peril, at all events did not exaggerate it. There is a sense of security engendered by long habit and familiarity with apparent danger, which renders a man mistrustful of the reality of that which has so often been shown to be a counterfeit. The inexperience of English statesmen suddenly transplanted to a new sphere of action often sees in the most ordinary political phenomena strange and alarming portents."

We, of course, can afford to smile now at the fears excited by French aggression; but looking at what Napoleon and his marshals had done, and remembering the apparent ease of Alexander's conquests in Asia, the presence of a grand French army on the Ganges did not seem an altogether impossible or improbable prospect.

The alliance between Russia and France, instead, however, of increasing the danger to British rule in the East, added to its security, by throwing Persia, whose whole hatred was directed against Russia for her encroaching policy on the Caspian, into the arms of England. England's right policy at that time seems clearer to us now than it did to the Home or British Indian Government. Our former policy had been to hold Persia as a buffer against our European enemies, the French, on the west, and to have her as a useful ally against Afghanistan on her eastern frontier. During the seven or eight years, however, since the last threat of Afghan invasion had been made, the Afghan Power had ceased to be formidable, owing to intestine quarrels. At the same time a new

Power—that of the Sikhs—was rising on our northern borders out of a dismembered province (the Panjab) of the once formidable Durani Empire. The Sikhs hated—and still hate—the Muhammadans, and hence the desirability of enlisting them on our side against the French and Persian confederacy, which was still believed to exist.

We have alluded already to the rival missions of Captain Malcolm and Sir Harford Jones, the one despatched by the British Indian, and the other by the English Government to the Court of Persia. The incidents of these missions are of interest at the present time, as they throw much light on the attitude which would be naturally taken by Persia at any time if England found herself—which God forbid!—at war with Russia. Captain Malcolm advanced very specious arguments for the occupation by England of the island of Karak, in the Persian Gulf. He urged that with an established footing there, which would soon become an emporium of our trade, we should be able to exclude other European Powers, and carry on whatever military operations we deemed consistent with and necessary to our honour and security. But British India then belonged to a trading company, and did not acknowledge an Empress as its ruler. Whether British honour and security have suffered by the neglect of Malcolm's advice will, of course, be answered differently by people holding different views on England's foreign policy.

In pursuance of the new policy, which consisted in an endeavour to unite the States of Afghanistan and the Panjab against the supposed Franco-Persian alliance—for it had not yet been seen that that alliance must fall to the ground on the reconciliation of Russia, Persia's enemy, to France—missions were sent to Cabul and Lahore, in September and October, 1808. It is thus just seventy years since Mr. Elphinstone set out in obedience to the then Governor-General, Lord Minto, to do at Cabul very much what Sir Neville Chamberlain would have tried to do for Lord Lytton, only in the former case the danger anticipated was from France, not Russia.

The necessity of including the Sikh ruler in the alliance that was desired no longer complicates the Indian Viceroy's policy. There is no "Lion of the Panjab" to be courted and conciliated now. British legions have swept away his magnificent Khalsa army, the modern representatives of his soldiers forming the finest of the Imperial troops; while his exiled descendant lives as an English nobleman on an estate in Norfolk, and is proud of being a friend of the Heir to the British Throne. Ranjit Sinh's provinces have long been administered by English commissioners and English magistrates, and could he revisit his capital, he would find an English

Lieutenant-Governor and a Chief-Court in possession.

It is as well to reflect now and then on the advance of England, as well as on that of Russia, if only to enable ourselves to see that an advancing Empire may not necessarily be wilfully aggressive, but may be forced by irresistible influences to extend its boundaries, and absorb semi-civilised and barbarous States on its borders, without this being any valid ground for apprehension on the part of a great European Power that may be doing the very same thing, under exactly the same impulses, elsewhere. When it comes, of course, to such a pass that both the Powers are standing with open jaws ready to swallow the last remaining independent State that lies between their immense territories, we get a condition of things for which it is difficult to find a precedent. In the absence of a "leading case," the parties that now divide English opinion on the "Afghan Question" would seem to think—the one that England should hasten to forestall her neighbour, and secure the by no means tempting morsel, and the other that there is no need for either Power to devour it, but that each can quite comfortably do with what it has already swallowed and is scarcely able to digest. This may be a rather vulgar way of putting it, savouring of the similes we have lately seen drawn of a thief holding a loaded pistol to a householder's head, and of the householder snatching up a baby to place it between himself and the thief; to which a reply was made, we believe, asking how would the matter of right stand if the thief held up a "loaded baby"—whether then the householder might strike it down without too delicate an inquiry into questions of international law.

Much advantage can rarely, however, be gained by far-fetched metaphorical arguments.

The Sikhs were still a Power in 1808—a young and rising Power—and Lord Minto had much difficulty to decide whether the best policy required him to curb the Sikhs, or to foster them as useful allies against the French. A middle course was pursued, and Mr. (afterwards Sir Charles) Metcalfe gained his spurs in diplomacy in carrying out this temporising policy. It was difficult, however, to enlist the sympathy of Ranjit Sinh for the danger to the British Empire in India from French aggression, and at the same time deny him the right he claimed of extending his rule over neighbouring States not in alliance with ourselves.

Shah Suja was now King of Afghanistan, having succeeded his brother, Zaman Shah, who had been dethroned and rendered blind by the Barakzai leader, Fateh Khan, in revenge for the death of the latter's father, which had been decreed by the King on the discovery of a treasonable plot against himself and his

Minister, in which Poinda Khan, the father of Fateh Khan and chief of the Barakzais, was implicated. The rise of these Barakzais to power commenced with this ill-judged severity on the part of Zaman Khan, whose family belonged to another branch—the Sadduzai—of the great Durani clan, of which both were branches.

The twenty-one sons of Poinda Khan seemed for a time to live only to avenge their father's death—revenge being an Afghan's first duty. That they rose—some at least among them, notably Dost Muhammad, the future Amir—was but an incidental consequence of the pursuit of their main object. For a full description of the varying fortunes of the Barakzai brothers we have not space at our command. Shah Suja for a time made head against them, but in June, 1809, was disastrously defeated, and had to withdraw beyond the frontier, barely, indeed, escaping with his life. The wanderings of Shah Suja and his many misfortunes; his futile attempts to regain his throne; his imprisonment in Cashmere by its governor, and afterwards in Lahore by Ranjit Sinh, to whom he lost the Koh-i-nur by a stratagem, the story of which has been often told,*—these are

---

* The trick was this: The Shah, for safety, carried the jewel in his turban, and Ranjit Sinh, having suggested an exchange of turbans, the unfortunate prince was obliged, by the law of courtesy, to comply.

recounted in Shah Suja's own autobiography, and will be found in some detail in Sir John Kaye's work. He found a resting-place and a pension in Ludhiana, in British territory, in 1816, and from that time until 1838, never ceased to entertain hopes of regaining his ancestral throne. These hopes were destined to be fulfilled, but with fatal result to himself and his patrons.

Before coming to the causes of the First Afghan War, which had for its direct object the restoration of Shah Suja to his throne, it is necessary to review the course of affairs in Afghanistan itself, and also the condition of things as they affected British Indian foreign policy.

Dost Muhammad, the most capable of the Barakzai brothers, had established himself firmly at Cabul, but Prince Kamran, of the old Saddozai family—the legitimate line—reigned supreme at Herat. Sultan Muhammad, a brother of Dost Muhammad, held Peshawar, and other brothers held Candahar. Thus mutilated, the Durani Empire seemed to have lost all its former menacing attitude towards India. On the contrary, however, in 1831, Peshawar fell to the Sikh ruler, Ranjit Sinh, and remained in his power until it passed with the rest of his dominions into British occupation.

The anxiety of Dost Muhammad to regain this province of Peshawar from the Sikhs became the great aim of his life, and he looked round to see on what allies he could trust for assistance. He found the Persians and English most suitable for this purpose, and, it is said, was willing, in 1837, to ally himself with either if he could be assured of aid against the Sihks.

In the autumn of 1837, however, rumours of two great events were heard, which vastly affected the future of Dost Muhammad and of others besides him. These were—a British envoy, Captain Burnes, came to Cabul as "commercial" resident, and Muhammad Shah, the Persian King, was laying siege to Herat.

Persia had been struggling against Russian aggression during the years intervening between 1810 and 1837. A period of outward observance of peace is included in this length of time, viz., from 1813 to 1826, but it was a hollow one, soon to be broken. A massacre of the isolated Russian garrisons and outposts in Gokchar brought down an avenging army, and so low was Persia reduced that, in 1828, she was compelled to cede Erivan and Nakhichevan, and consent to the Russians drawing their frontier-line considerably eastward. An indemnity to Russia of eighty millions of roubles was also stipulated for. Thus was Persia "delivered, bound hand and foot, to the Court of St. Petersburg."

The English policy pursued at this time has been severely criticised, as we appear to have purchased a release from engagements which bound us to assist the Persians against Russia. The result was the immense advance of Russian influence at the Court of Persia, the heir-apparent having, it is said, married a Russian princess, and adopted the Christian faith. Then began the policy of making Persia play Russia's game. It became the object of Russia to use the resources of Persia in furtherance of her own ends, without overt action on her part, thereby avoiding a collision with other European Powers, whose jealousy it was her aim not to arouse. The first outcome of this new Russian move was an encroachment by Persia on Khorasan. It became the common talk of the bazaars of Khorasan, Afghanistan, and even of Bombay, that an allied Russian and Persian army would march upon Herat, Cabul, and India.

In 1836, the Herat campaign commenced, and the story of the memorable siege of that city deserves to be read by all who would know what is the value of one brave Englishman in a cause upon which he had set his heart.

It may be safely affirmed that Herat would have fallen to the Persian King if it had not been for the courage and firmness of Eldred Pottinger, a young English officer, who found his way to Herat just as the Persians began their attack.

On the 23rd November, 1837, the siege of Herat actually began, and continued until the 9th of September of the following year.

Herat is described as surrounded by a fair expanse of country, filled with cornfields, vineyards, and gardens; little fortified villages studded the plain, and the bright waters of small running streams lightened the pleasant landscape. The beauty of Herat was, however, without the walls; within, all was dirt and desolation. Strongly fortified on every side by a wet ditch, and a solid outer wall, with five gates, each defended by a small outwork, the city presented but few claims to the admiration of the traveller. Herat was divided into four quarters, consisting of four long bazaars, roofed with arched brickwork, meeting in a small domed quadrangle in the centre of the city. The total population is estimated as having been about 45,000. Mosques and caravanserais, public baths and public reservoirs, varied the wretched uniformity of the narrow, dirty streets, and these were roofed across so as to be little better than dark tunnels, where every conceivable description of dirt collected and putrified. When wonder was expressed by Arthur Conolly that people could live in such filth, the reply was, "The climate is fine, and if dirt killed people, where would the Afghans be?"

The picture drawn by Kaye of the political and moral condition of the people of Herat, forms a fitting counterpart to the description of the outward imperfections of the city. Every kind of cruelty and vice, and every form of tyranny and misrule, seem to have been concentrated here; and if ever a clean sweep of a city and its inhabitants seemed likely to be a matter of small loss to the rest of the human race, it might have appeared so in the case of Herat.

But high moral character and honesty are not necessary concomitants of valour and martial prowess, although even these qualities are not the worse for being conjoined with the former. One man, at least, in Herat, possessed all these qualifications, and he saved Herat. It would be unfair, however, to leave it to be supposed that the besieging army of the Persians was much, if at all, superior to the Heratis in those moral qualities in which the latter were so wanting. But the Persian King's troops were infinitely better soldiers, and quite as brave men as the Afghans. Their non-success was the fault of their leaders, while opposed to them was an English officer, who showed himself worthy to rank with some of the best generals of his country, but who had devoted himself to the cause of the besieged simply as a volunteer.

Russian officers aided the Persians at Herat, and Russian diplomatists urged them to the expedition. It was a natural conclusion that, so encouraging and so aiding Persia, Russia had ulterior designs not wholly unconnected with thoughts of the British Empire in India. It is certain that such was the feeling of the English Ministry. But when an explanation was desired by Lord Durham from the Russian Minister of conduct so contrary to the declarations of the Czar's Government, the reply was that if Count Simonich, the Russian Minister at the Court of Persia, had encouraged the Persian King to proceed against Herat, he had acted in direct violation of his instructions. This, however, was but an early example of that persistent course of encroachment in Central Asia which Russian generals and diplomatists have carried out in direct contravention of the instructions they are said to have received from St. Petersburg.

While the siege of Herat was in progress, Captain Burnes had been prosecuting his "commercial" mission at Cabul at the Court of Dost Muhammad, the Amir or ruler of that part of Afghanistan. The Amir was believed, however, to be intriguing with the Persians for their assistance in a projected war against the Sikhs to recover Peshawar. To the English in India the security of the Anglo-Indian Empire seemed in 1837-38, to be threatened both from within and without. From Nepal to Burma the Native States were evincing signs of feverish interest in the advance of what they supposed was a Muhammadan invasion from beyond the Afghan frontier. Public securities declined in value, and the rumour spread from mouth to mouth that the Company's reign was nearly at an end.

To the high officers of the British Indian Government matters appeared somewhat differently, but were sufficiently black. Herat was being besieged by the Persian King-of-Kings, Russian officers were directing the siege, the Barakzai Sirdars, including Dost Muhammad, were intriguing with Persia. It seemed probable, therefore, that having taken Herat, the Persian King would either push on his conquests to Cabul and Candahar, or render Dost Muhammad the vassal of Persia by aiding him against the Sikhs, and thereby make Afghanistan the basis of future operations to be undertaken not only by the Persians themselves, but by them jointly with the Russians, who were now their allies.

It was then the true policy of the British Government to keep Afghanistan independent, and to cement a friendly alliance with its ruler or rulers. This, broadly, was the aim of Lord Auckland in all the diplomacy that followed.

We have now arrived at the threshold of the First Afghan War, which arose directly out of this policy, the ostensible object of which was, it must be remembered, to make Afghanistan independent, if possible, or as much as possible, but at any rate friendly to British interests—to prevent its falling into the hands of the Persians, and through them into that of the Russians; to be used as a weapon against the British Empire in India.

CHAPTER VII.

THE FIRST AFGHAN WAR.

Lord Auckland's Policy in 1837—Case for Dost Muhammad Stated by Sir John Kaye—Afghan Ideas of Hereditary Claims to Sovereignty—The Tripartite Treaty—The Army of the Indus—Passage Through Sindh Delayed—Appointment of Macnaghten as Political Officer with the Expedition—English Gold Scattered Freely—Shah Suja's Reception at Candahar—Assault and Capture of Ghazni—Massacre of the Ghazis —Flight of Dost Muhammad beyond the Hindu Kush—Failure of Pursuit through Treachery of Haji Khan—Intrinsic Weakness of Shah Suja's Course Demonstrated—Cost of Living for English Officers at Cabul—Kaye's Judgment of the British " System " introduced into Afghanistan—Honours to the Victors—Designs of Further Interference Westwards—The Story of Colonel Stoddart and Arthur Conolly's "Missions"—Their Cruel Fate—Lord Ellenborough's Letter to the Amir of Bokhara—Brief Review of "The Afghan Tragedy" of 1838-42—Story of Dr. Brydon's Escape.

IT is easy to be wise after the event. It is clear to every one now that Lord Auckland's mode of carrying out the policy of making Afghanistan a free and independent State, to act as a buffer against Persia and Russia, was not the wisest plan to effect that object, and did indeed result in making that State bitterly hostile and independent, not through our aid, but, it may be said, in spite of it. In 1837, however, matters were not so plain to the eyes of statesmen, whose days and nights were made anxious by the rumours of great preparations across the frontier, while the internal sources of disquiet were not few.

It was believed, whether rightly or wrongly may now be questioned, that Dost Muhammad was not likely to be a sincere friend to the English, however ostensibly so he might appear. In the words of the Simla manifesto, he and his brothers were "ill-fitted, under any circumstances, to be useful allies to the British." Sir John Kaye has ably stated the case for Dost Muhammad. He has shown that that prince really wished for the English alliance, and only waited for some consideration to be shown to his wishes with regard to Peshawar; the restoration of which province he claimed from the Sikhs, and hoped to regain by our intercession. In that case he would have abandoned Russia and Persia at once. It did not suit Lord Auckland's policy to alienate the Sikhs by pressing Dost Muhammad's claims, even if he had believed in Dost Muhammad's sincerity. It must be remembered, too, that Dost Muhammad was in possession only of Cabul and Ghazni, Candahar and Herat being in possession, the former of his brother, and the latter of a Saddozai prince. To have a series of disjointed kingdoms or chieftainships in Afghanistan, involving a separate consideration of the interests of each, and all the trouble of conciliating rival princes, seemed naturally enough less favourable to the policy Lord Auckland had adopted than the consolidation of the whole under one King. Some idea of Dost Muhammad's position being that of a usurper doubtless contributed to the determination to inaugurate a policy which was as startling as it was novel. This was no other than to put forward the exile, Shah Suja, the former legitimate King of the Afghans, who had been driven out, as before explained, by Dost Muhammad and his brothers, in pursuance of a family feud that arose from the deaths of Poinda Khan and Fateh Khan, at the hands of Zaman Shah and Prince Kamran respectively. To restore Shah Suja, the rightful sovereign, to the throne of his ancestors, did not seem so wrongful a proceeding then as it does to us now. It was believed that the Afghans would welcome their King if once the strength of the Barakzai family were broken. The Duranis had been terribly oppressed by Dost Muhammad, and it was supposed they would flock to Shah Suja's standard. But it has been since learnt how little the Afghans regard legitimacy and the hereditary rights of royal houses. Their notions of sovereignty have little in common with refined Western ideas of it. The strongest is the one whom they willingly acknowledge as King. A fatal objection, too, to the restored monarch was the fact that he had come back to them as a puppet in the hands of the infidels, and that his power rested on no more national basis than British bayonets and British gold. It would be tedious and of little use to enter at length into all the workings of that policy which we have briefly sketched above. A tripartite treaty was signed between the British Indian Government, Ranjit Sinh, the Sikh ruler of the Panjab, and Shah Suja. The Sikhs were to co-operate in the restoration of Shah Suja to the throne of Cabul, and the King's eldest son was to march with a Sikh army from Peshawar through the Khaibar Pass, while Shah Suja himself, with some levies of his own, but accompanied by an English army of mixed European and Sepoy soldiers, on which the brunt of the campaign would fall, marched through the Bolan Pass, to Quettah, and thence to Candahar. Sir John Keane (afterwards Lord Keane of Ghazni) led the Bombay column, and Sir Willoughby Cotton commanded the Southern Army, called the Army of the Indus, which set out from Firozpur, on the Indus, on the 10th December, 1837. This army consisted of about 9,500 men, and 38,000 camp-followers. Thirty-thousand baggage camels, well-laden, accompanied them. On the 14th January the army entered Sindh. It was the 16th of March before it reached Dadar, at the mouth of the Bolan Pass. It had been delayed by difficulties in Sindh, which was not then British territory. The Amirs of that country required a good deal of over-aweing before they would grant a passage to our troops. The privations undergone by the army in its march across the desert were extreme. The distance from Shikarpur to Dadar is 146 miles. It was accomplished by the Bengal column in sixteen painful marches. Water and forage were so scarce that the cattle suffered terribly on the way. The camels fell dead by scores on the desert, and further on the Baluchi robbers carried them off with appalling dexterity. When they reached cultivated land the green crops were used as forage for the horses.

Sir John Keane with the Bombay Army had landed at Vikkur at the end of November, but was compelled, from the hostility of the Sindh rulers, to remain inactive till December 24th. On the 4th of April he reached Quettah, to take command of the expedition now increased by the Bombay column, which had made a long and difficult march through Sindh. As the expedition had for its object the restoration of a King and the pacification of his country, it was deemed desirable to send with it a civil officer, as representative of the Governor-General of India. The choice of Lord Auckland fell upon Mr. W. H. (afterwards Sir William) Macnaghten, then Foreign Secretary with the Government of India, a man of great abilities, an eminent Oriental scholar, and withal fully imbued with the spirit of Lord Auckland with regard to the affair in hand ; unless, as some think, it were more correct to say that he had infused his spirit and sentiments into Lord Auckland.

Despite the difficulties in the way of supplies, and the loss of beasts of burden, the army reached Candahar without serious opposition, although a small but resolute band of the enemy might have barred their way at the Bolan Pass, and perhaps effectually repelled the invading forces with disaster. There is no doubt that English money was largely used to buy off the adherents of the Barakzais. The Afghans discovered that the gold of the Feringhees was as serviceable as other gold, and Afghan allegiance was purchased to a large extent. The system of corruption thus commenced could not but involve the invaders in difficulty afterwards, when the treasure-chest became exhausted.

Shah Suja's entrance into Candahar was more remarkable for the curiosity than for the enthusiasm displayed. Macnaghten interpreted the demonstration in the most favourable light, and saw an unclouded prospect of success in the future. And so for a time it seemed. Ghazni was taken by assault, with an ease that seemed marvellous to the Afghans, seeing that Sir John Keane had no heavy guns with him. Treachery, however, on the part of the enemy aided as much as British bayonets. One of the Barakzai nobles—the nephew of Dost Muhammad—

turned traitor, and gave information which enabled Sir John Keane's engineers to blow up part of the walls of Ghazni by gunpowder, and so effect an entrance, and the capture of the city. Shah Suja showed his capacity for conciliating his subjects by ordering the slaughter in cold blood of fifty Ghazis, who were taken prisoners. These fanatics court death in battle, but the massacre of them in cold blood was in the highest degree impolitic, to say nothing of the inhumanity of the deed. "That martyrdom," says Kaye, "was never forgotten. The day of reckoning came at last; and when our unholy policy sank buried in blood and ashes, the shrill cry of the Ghazis sounded as its funeral wail." He refers, of course, to that terrible death-struggle some two years later, of the retreating army in the passes of the Khurd-Cabul, when the Ghazis rushed in, hungry for the blood of the infidels, and completed the slaughter of the survivors.

At Ghazni Brigadier Sale, who afterwards became famous at Jalalabad, commanded the main column, and greatly distinguished himself. Although the capture of this city was not marked by the worst feature of war—for the women were not ill-treated—the carnage was terrible. Upwards of 500 of the garrison were buried by the besiegers, besides those who fell beyond the walls; the victors losing only seventeen killed and 165 wounded; 1,600 prisoners were taken, and immense stores of grain, many horses, and numerous arms.

After a futile attempt at negotiation, Dost Muhammad, seeing that resistance was hopeless—for his own followers were deserting him, or were lukewarm in their support—mounted his horse at Urghandi, a few miles to the west of Cabul, whither he had gone out to dispute the progress of the invaders, and, with a few followers, turned his face towards the regions of the Hindu Kush.

On the 2nd of August Dost Muhammad fled, and on the following day the British army, which was marching upon Cabul, heard the news, and a party of horsemen set out in pursuit. Haji Khan Kakar, a man of mean origin, who had risen to be an Afghan chief, offered to lead the pursuit. He was all the while, however, in treasonable correspondence with Dost Muhammad, and did all he could to misdirect the English officers. The pursuit failed, the Amir escaped beyond the mountains, and Haji Khan suffered for his treachery by banishment as a State prisoner to Chunar.

On the 7th of August Shah Suja and a British army entered Cabul, the former, after an absence of thirty years, the latter for the first time. He had been restored to his throne by the money-bags and the bayonets of the British; but it was a hopeless task to attempt to keep him on it. He had fallen once miserably, and not even English soldiers and Indian rupees could set him up permanently again. He might have succeeded without the assistance of the hated infidels, but the knowledge that they, and they only, supported him on his tottering throne alienated even those who would naturally favour the lineal descendant of the famous Ahmad Shah.

It was no part of the original programme that an English army should remain in occupation of the Afghan capital and country; but it soon became manifest that the puppet we had set up would not be able to retain his throne without extraneous aid. So Macnaghten remained as British Envoy, and the Bengal column remained as well.

On the 18th of September the Bombay troops commenced their return march to India through the Kojak and the Bolan Passes. Those who stayed behind were disappointed, for, says Kaye, "a country, in which wine was selling at the price of 300 rupees (£30) a dozen, and cigars at a rupee (2s.) a-piece, was not one in which the officers of the army were likely to desire to pitch their tents for a sojourn of any long continuance." A small detachment, however, of the Bengal troops afterwards returned to India, under Sir John Keane, leaving the rest under Sir Willoughby Cotton in occupation of Afghanistan. Then began the system of planting small detachments of British troops in isolated positions throughout the country; which was, in the opinion of some, one of the great errors that marked our sojourn in Afghanistan.

The unpopularity of Shah Suja grew daily more manifest, but the people seemed to have settled down into something like quiescence under the reign of English gold, for cupidity is one of their strongest passions. They hated the Feringhees, but did not refuse their gold. The old experience, which we had seen so often in our relations with the States of India, began to be felt. British bayonets were employed to execute the orders of the Shah and his officers. Bound by treaty not to interfere with the internal affairs of the country, they had to permit, and even aid in enforcing, much that was unjust. Says Sir John Kaye, " It would have been a miracle if such a system had not soon broken down with a desolating crash, and buried its authors in the ruins." The more we surrounded Shah Suja with our authority the less firmly was he seated on the throne. Meanwhile, the successes of the recent campaign brought honours to the chief actors. Lord Auckland was created an earl; Sir John Keane became Baron Keane of Ghazni; Mr. Macnaghten was made a baronet; Colonel Wade (who had led the force through the Khaibar) a knight; and brevets and Bath honours were numerous.

The extent to which our success in Afghanistan

had encouraged designs of further interference with the Powers to the west of Cabul can be understood only by a reference to the correspondence of Sir W. Macnaghten, and other high Anglo-Indian officers, during the brief occupation of Afghan territory by a British army. Not only did Macnaghten advise an attack upon Herat, which was "giving trouble," and its annexation to Shah Suja's dominions, but missions were sent to Bokhara, Khokand, and Khiva. Colonel Stoddart, indeed, had been at Bokhara ever since the close of 1838, having been sent by the English Minister at the Court of Persia to obtain the release of some Russians who were in captivity there, and also to conclude a friendly treaty with the Amir of Bokhara. The story is well known of Stoddart's imprisonment, in violation of all the laws that regulate international intercourse—but what do barbarous Khans and Amirs know of such?—of the gross and wanton cruelties practised upon him, and of his final atrocious murder. Arthur Conolly fared no better. He started from Cabul in the autumn of 1840, ostensibly on a mission to Khiva and Khokand. Thence, on an invitation of the Amir of Bokhara, he proceeded to that city, where he found Stoddart in a state of captivity, but more honourable and less painful than that which he had been condemned to suffer during part of the preceding years. One of Conolly's reasons for visiting Bokhara was, it is said, to induce Stoddart to recant the profession of Muhammadanism he had made. He found, on his arrival, that poor Stoddart's conversion had been effected by such gentle means as incarceration in a pit full of vermin and filth. His grave, too, was dug, with the threat that unless he professed the faith of Islam he would be buried alive in it. Conolly found he had only been decoyed into a trap to undergo similar treatment, and was in the end subjected to the same fate as Stoddart suffered. It is believed that both died by the hand of the public executioner, but the precise period of their death is doubtful. Native accounts make it the 17th of June, 1842 ; and manuscripts written by Arthur Conolly himself and despatched to Cabul bring up the sad narrative of his sufferings to the 24th of May of that year. On the 28th of May Stoddart despatched an official letter to the Indian Government, which was forwarded with Conolly's journals. The neglect of the Government they served so faithfully embittered the hard fate of these officers. It was after their death that Lord Ellenborough wrote a letter to the Amir of Bokhara, in which he described them as "innocent travellers," and as such requested their release. Kaye rightly says that had they been then living, such a repudiation of their official character would have sealed their fate, as it practically proclaimed them to be spies. Let us hope this is no precedent to be followed in the case of other officers of Government who may fall into the clutches of barbarous rulers, when serving their country. Kaye describes the fate of these officers as "a painful episode in the epic of the Afghan war." It was so, truly.

The Afghan tragedy is conveniently divided into three periods, the first of which ends with the restoration of Shah Suja to the throne of Cabul on the 7th August, 1839. The second period embraces those two years of Shah Suja's short reign, during which he was kept on his throne only by British bayonets and British gold; the events which led to the insurrection of the Afghan tribes against the Feringhee infidels, as they called the English; the subsequent difficulties arising, it is now believed, more from the divided authority and incapable commanders of the British than from the strength of the enemy; and the crowning disasters of the retreat from Cabul and massacre of the whole Cabul division of the British army and its camp-followers, with the exception of about a hundred prisoners and *one* man, Dr. Brydon, who effected his escape, in a condition more dead than alive, to Jalalabad, which he reached on 13th January, 1842. The third and last period is occupied with the march of the avenging army that was slowly collected and despatched under General Pollock from Peshawar to effect a junction with General Nott's division, which had been shut up in

Candahar during the winter, but which now commenced that extraordinary "withdrawal" to the plains of India *viâ* Ghazni, Cabul, Jalalabad, and Peshawar, which looked so remarkably like an advance, that Kaye has rightly designated it as a retirement "unparalleled, perhaps, in the political history of the world." The punishment inflicted upon those deemed guilty of any participation in the previous disasters to the British arms, more especially upon the tribes concerned in the massacre of the retreating British army, was, perhaps, sufficiently severe, and read the Afghans a lesson which they did not soon forget. The English prisoners, too, who had almost concluded that they had been abandoned by the Government to their fate, were recovered after adventures more thrilling and escapes more wonderful than anything to be found in fiction. The policy of withdrawal was eventually carried out, and Afghanistan left to its own people in December 1842, after more than four years of deep anxiety caused by our wilful interference with its rude politics.

To give anything approaching to an exhaustive account of these events would far exceed our present intention, and Sir John Kaye's masterly work on the Afghan War renders it unnecessary to do so. In his pages the student of Indian history will never cease to find delight, for the clear and incisive judgment which he has brought to bear upon the difficult ques-

The First Afghan War. 151

tions of policy that then arose leaves little to be desired. The Afghans could have wished no fairer or more impartial chronicler, while the present generation of Englishmen may thank him for having cleared up what was dubious, even where it involved proving, as in so many instances it did, that our own action was indefensible.

A correspondent of the *Daily News*, subscribing himself " H.J.R.L.," sent the following interesting account of the escape of Dr. Brydon, the sole survivor of the Cabul force, who found his way to Jalalabad, to tell the sad story of its fate. " H.J.R.L.'s " account agrees substantially with that given by Sir John Kaye. He says :—

" Dr. Brydon was the doctor of my old regiment. His pleasant face and rotund figure always made it the more difficult to realise that he was the only survivor of that terrible retreat, of which he was most reluctant to speak. It was towards the end of the Cabul Pass that a few survivors had struggled. Among them was the native doctor of Brydon's then regiment. Calling Brydon to him, he said, ' Doctor Sahib, I cannot possibly escape; I am dying from cold and hunger. Take my pony, and do the best you can for yourself.' Brydon tried to encourage the poor man, but, seeing that he was indeed dying, he took the pony, and through the confusion forced his way to the front. There he found a small group of mounted officers, who, knowing they were just at the end of the Pass, where it opens out on the plain on which Jalalabad stands, had determined to make a push for life. Seeing Brydon on this wretched, half-starved pony, they declared they could not possibly wait for him, as any delay might cause their utter destruction. On they went, leaving Brydon slowly toiling after them. The Afghans saw this group approaching, met and slew every man; then, thinking no one else was coming, went back to the hills. Just then Brydon passed.

"At Jalalabad the greatest anxiety prevailed as to the whereabouts of General Elphinstone's force, no news having come through the Pass, though it was known he was retreating, when one evening a man, slowly riding a worn-out pony, was descried at the entrance of the Pass. Some cavalry were sent to bring him in. It was Brydon, the only survivor. As he entered the gate he fell senseless from fatigue. When he came to himself his first question was about the pony that had saved his life. It was dead.

"When Brydon told me the story we were walking home one night from mess, under the solemn calm of an Indian night. He bade me put my finger into the mark left by an Afghan sabre, which, glancing from a book he had put into his forage cap, had sliced a piece of the skull clean out.

"Brydon took part in the defence of Jalalabad as one of the 'illustrious garrison,' and, strangely enough, lived to take part in the defence of Lucknow."

CHAPTER VIII.

AFGHAN AFFAIRS AFTER THE WAR OF 1838—42.

The Real Cause of the Damage to England's Position in Central Asia from the Cabul Disaster—Lord Ellenborough's Policy in 1842—Native Views on the Evacuation of Afghanistan—Rawlinson's Opinion of the Afghans as Soldiers—England "The Burnt Child," and Afghanistan "The Fire"—Internal Affairs of Afghanistan between the Retreat of General Elphinstone and the Advance of General Pollock—Muhammad Shah Khan a Noble Exception to the Generality of the Afghans—Murder of Shah Suja, the Puppet-King—Accession of Fatih Jang—Akbar Khan Intrigues for Power—Fall of Fatih Jang—Proclamation of Shuhpur—Lord Ellenborough's "Song of Triumph"—Policy with Regard to Dost Muhammad Khan—England's Afghan Policy from 1842 to 1852—Origin of the Persian War of 1856—Herat and Treaty of Paris of 1857—Virtual Disregard of Treaty by Persia—Dost Muhammad's Neutrality in 1856-58 Purchased—Policy of Subsidies Discussed—Cost of Afghan War—The Blood Feud between the Afghans and the English—Sir John Lawrence's Treaties with Dost Muhammad—Extent of Dost Muhammad's Dominions—He Subdues Candahar and Herat—His Death—Subsequent Anarchy in Afghanistan—Rival Claimants to the "Masnad"—Shere Ali, the Designated Successor—His Son, Yakub Khan, is Made Governor of Herat—Afzul Khan Obtains Possession of Cabul, and is Proclaimed Amir—Shere Ali's Defeat—Yakub Khan's Gallant Achievements—Shere Ali Restored in 1868—He Suspects Yakub Khan of Treachery—Yakub Demands to be Acknowledged Heir-Apparent—Open Quarrel Between the Amir and Yakub—Yakub's Flight—Reconciliation and Imprisonment—Other Claimants to the Succession.

IT was not so much our retirement from Afghanistan, in 1842, as the conditions under which it was carried out that injured British *prestige* and disparaged England's position in all Central Asia. If, after recovering the prisoners, our officers had remained for another year in the country; and then, in an orderly and honourable manner, after a suitable arrangement with the native authorities into whose hands we might have thought it fitting to resign the government, we had withdrawn from Afghan soil, the effects of our previous disasters would have been mitigated, if not entirely removed. But Lord Ellenborough was too anxious to rescue the armies of Generals Pollock and Nott from what he considered to be their critical position in an intensely hostile country, hardly capable of furnishing supplies, always at their wits' end for carriage, and oppressed with the recollection of the fate that had so recently befallen their predecessors, to let delicate consideration of the honour of the English name weigh with him against the terrible dangers his imagination saw in a further occupation of Afghanistan.

Indeed, it was at one time possible—nay, so probable as to be deemed by some almost certain—that the fears of the Governor-General would so far paralyse his judgment that a distinct refusal would be given to Pollock to advance on Cabul " to assist the retreat of the Candahar force " as it was the fashion officially to style that wonderful " retirement on the plains of India viâ Ghazni, Cabul, and Peshawar," to which we have already referred.

What really happened in the end, as the result of Lord Ellenborough's policy, was that after reading the natives certain "lessons" the British army retired precipitately from Afghan territory without any understanding having been come to with the Durani chiefs, and pursued, indeed, by an implacable foe—generally, but not always, at a respectful distance—down to the last pass debouching on the plains. Thus no doubt can be entertained that the previous ill effects on our reputation were considerably enhanced; the general native idea being, both in India and in Central Asia, that we were in reality driven from the mountains. Nor has the belief been uncommon among our own officers that in retiring from Afghanistan we yielded to superior strength; whereas, in truth, never was the country more thoroughly in our power during the whole period from the commencement of the Afghan War than at the moment of our retreat.

It has been asserted on the highest authority, that, except during the fatal winter of 1841-42, when by a concurrence of the most unforeseen events, our forces at Cabul had become utterly demoralised, the Afghans were never able to make a successful stand, even for an hour, against either British soldiers or Indian Sepoys. Sir Henry Rawlinson declared in

1875 that no officer who served through the Afghan War would hesitate to meet the whole assembled forces of Cabul and Candahar combined with a single brigade of British troops; and even in mountain warfare, where the Afghan marksman with his "jazail" (or rifled matchlock) had formerly an undoubted superiority over "old Brown Bess," the substitution of the breechloading rifle has now redeemed our only weakness. Whether Sir Henry Rawlinson would be willing to commit himself to such a statement in the fall of 1878, after the recent information we have received of the state of the Amir's army, drilled, it is alleged, in part at least, by Russian officers, and with the arsenals of Russia, as it is also asserted, to select from, we have no means of deciding. We opine from the much larger forces which it has been deemed necessary to assemble on the north-west frontier that it is not the opinion of high military authorities in India that the Afghans are such contemptible enemies as Sir Henry Rawlinson, in 1875 at least, supposed. The object, we should observe, which Sir Henry Rawlinson had in making the above observation was not to encourage the idea of our again ascending the passes, but rather to correct the erroneous impression which he believed to be generally entertained of the military strength of Afghanistan, and the consequent overestimate that might be made of the difficulties which would lie in the way of a Russian advance upon India from any opposition the Afghans themselves could interpose.

We propose in this and the succeeding chapters of this book to trace very rapidly, but with as much succinctness as may be, the relations between Afghanistan and the British Indian Government from the evacuation of that country in 1842 to the present time. This will enable us to consider with more advantage, perhaps, the causes that may have led to the present complications, and to estimate the value, from various standpoints, of the very opposite opinions that have been called forth upon what will now take its place in history as "the Afghan question of 1878," unless a deeper significance should accrue to it, demanding a more comprehensive and far-reaching title.

For a number of years after the Afghan War we imitated the "burnt child," and studiously avoided all intercourse with the country that had been the scene of our disasters.

The three independent Governments of Cabul, Candahar, and Herat, that had been in existence before our advent, again asserted their rule. Persia had too much occupation at home to interfere with her eastern neighbour.

Sir John Kaye, in his admirable work on the Afghan War, has collected from various sources all that is known of the internal affairs of Afghanistan after the departure of the ill-fated Cabul column, which marched forth to destruction under General Elphinstone on the 6th of January, 1842, and before the arrival of General Pollock with the avenging army. Of the wretched puppet-King we had set up in the place of the really capable Dost Muhammad, we know that he remained for a time nominal ruler of Cabul, to the astonishment indeed of those who believed that the insurrection which had caused the expulsion of the English had been as much directed against Shah Suja as against his Feringhee patrons. The fact was that the chiefs dreaded the vengeance of the English for the fearful injuries dealt to them, and felt that Shah Suja was the only one that was ever likely to stand between them and that vengeance. Of Shah Suja's conduct various opinions have been held, some believing that he was the original fomenter of the insurrection, but that he intended it only to attain such dimensions as would compel his English patrons to remain and support him against his enemies; while others suppose that he was sincerely friendly to the English, but weak and incapable to the last degree. There is no doubt, however, that one Afghan Prince, Muhammad Zaman Khan, was a noble exception to the mass of his countrymen; for while the independence of his country was dear to him, he never stained his patriotism with those foul crimes in which others delighted; and it is recorded of him that nothing could exceed the kindness of this old man to the English hostages, who found a sanctuary in his house. He even raised and paid from his limited resources a force of 3,000 men, chiefly for the protection of his English guests, or (as they were really) prisoners. This Nawab had been made Vazir or Minister of Shah Suja; but soon dissensions broke out among the rival factions, and mutual distrust prevented concerted action. Shah Suja was murdered by the son of the Nawab, against the wish, and notwithstanding the efforts, of the old man to save him; and the body of the wretched King, after it had been stripped of its royal apparel and ornaments, was flung into a ditch. His death was the consummation of the fierce strife that had been raging between Shah Suja and the Barakzai princes for forty years.

The second son of Shah Suja, Fatih Jang, was now raised to the throne, and he condoned the murder of his father on the ground that it was no time for avenging private family wrongs when all ought to make common cause against the infidels. But the Barakzais were not likely with patience to see the son of their hated rival seated on the throne. Civil war soon raged in the city; and Akbar Khan, who had remained at a distance with the majority of the English prisoners still in his possession, waiting to see how matters went at the capital, now marched on Cabul. Akbar Khan, it will be remembered, was the son of Dost Muhammad, and is known to history as the murderer of the English Envoy, Sir William Macnaghten, at a conference held near the walls of the cantonments at Cabul, just previous to their evacuation. This prince, whose character seems to have been a strange mixture of ferocity and sensibility, besieged Fatih Jang, the unfortunate young King, in the Bala Hissar, or citadel of Cabul, and when, at last, the place was taken, began himself to exercise regal power by the usual Afghan device of keeping the nominal sovereign as a puppet. He found it convenient to support, as titular prince, this Saddozai youth, Fatih Jang, because the Nawab, Muhammad Zaman Khan, of his own (Barakzai) tribe, also claimed to be King of the Afghans. The good Nawab, who had so nobly protected the English captives, was defeated in battle, owing to the desertion of his followers, and was made most reluctantly to give up his prisoners, whom he had treated as guests, to the High Priest, Mir Haji. From his custody they were soon transferred—sold, we should rather say—to Akbar Khan, who thus obtained possession of the persons of all the English who had been taken captive before and after the massacre. His object in doing this was to make good terms for himself on the return of the English with an avenging army—an event he fully expected. Fatih Jang was driven from his throne by Akbar Khan as soon as the latter had possessed himself of the treasure,* to which Fatih Khan had succeeded on Shah Suja's death—treasure which had been amassed from the subsidies drawn from the Indian Government. Fatih Jang had escaped in rags and tatters to the camp of General Pollock, as that officer, with the army of vengeance, was approaching Cabul. Following General Pollock to the capital, he was reinstalled on his throne, but was emphatically told that the English had had enough of supporting puppet-Kings at Cabul, and he must now shift for himself. When he learnt this, he peremptorily refused to wear the crown, and begged to be allowed to accompany Pollock's camp to India, a request which was granted both to him and the old blind King, Zaman Shah, who had now a second time to find refuge in British territory. Another King, named Shahpur, of the same unlucky Saddozai family, was proclaimed on the day Pollock was leaving Cabul, but it was a mere mockery, for he was dethroned again before the British forces reached India.

After Lord Ellenborough had proclaimed the

* About £200,000.

victory of the English troops in his famous proclamation of the Gates, called by the Duke of Wellington a "Song of Triumph"—than which no document that ever emanated from the bureau of a statesman has been more ridiculed and censured for its bombosity and folly—it became necessary to decide what should be done with Dost Muhammad Khan, who was, it will be remembered, a prisoner along with his family in our hands. We had decreed and carried out his dethronement; and, deserted by his followers, and feeling how hopeless was his resistance to British might, he had surrendered himself to Sir W. Macnaghten, by whom he was honourably treated, and forwarded as a State prisoner to Calcutta. It is unnecessary here to detail the intrigues which followed the first departure of the English from Cabul. Suffice it to say that when Dost Muhammad found his way back to his capital, he was not long in regaining his former authority as Amir, and Akbar Khan became his Vazir, or Chief Minister. From that time to 1852 we carefully avoided any interference with Afghan affairs. In that year, however, died Yar Muhammad Khan, the notorious Minister of Shah Kamran of Herat, who had, with the aid of Eldred Pottinger, successfully conducted the siege of that city against the Persian host in 1837-38. Persia would gladly have taken advantage of the confusion that followed upon the Vazir's death to again attempt the reduction of Herat. This, however we prevented by threatening to suspend diplomatic relations, and so compelled the Shah into a convention by which he bound himself not to make any future attack upon Afghan territory. This committed us, doubtless, to hostilities with Persia in the event of her breaking the convention, but it was deemed imperative to prevent Herat falling into her hands, chiefly because it was feared she might exchange that city with Russia for Erivan, or some other place. This doctrine—that Herat must be independent of Russia and Persia—has been a political maxim with most English statesmen ever since.

In 1856 the contingency which had been foreseen occurred, and Persian troops were sent to occupy Herat, and did succeed temporarily in doing so. The war with England followed upon this action—there were other causes, but this was the most important—during the course of which Persia thought it prudent to abandon its conquest; and at the Peace of Paris, concluded in 1857, special provisions regarding Herat were inserted in the Treaty—an evidence of our traditional dread of Russia. The wisdom of the provision which burdened us with the liability to attack Persia the moment she marched eastward has been much questioned. Still more has the barren stipulation against the Shah's interference with the Government of Herat been adversely criticised. That this latter one was futile soon became evident, for Sultan Ahmad Khan, a nephew of Dost Muhammad, who was a refugee at Teheran when the Treaty of Paris was concluded, was sent by the Persian Shah to assume the reins of Government immediately upon the withdrawal of the Persian garrison from Herat, and he remained for the next five years in undisguised dependence upon Persia, although his independence was proclaimed, in deference to their obligations, by both the British Government and the Shah. A Russian mission, under M. Khannikof, which visited Herat in 1858, succeeded in completing the dependency of Sultan Ahmad upon Persia. In 1857 the great importance was seen of securing the neutrality of the Amir Dost Muhammad during the Persian War and the Indian Mutinies, when the fate of our Indian Empire seemed trembling in the balance. We, therefore, for once stepped aside from the policy of non-interference which had been pursued for fifteen years, and sent a friendly mission to Afghanistan under Major Lumsden. Our officers proceeded only to Candahar, but succeeded in purchasing the Amir's goodwill for a subsidy of a lakh of rupees (£10,000) per mensem, to be continued as long as his services might be of advantage to us.

Of the morality of this bargain, Sir Henry Rawlinson remarks that it may appear questionable, and of the terms, he admits that they may seem exorbitant to English politicians, but, he adds, " when work is to be done, subsidies are still the rule in the East, and experience has ever shown that true economy consists in paying well, or not at all." In this case the "work" stipulated for in return for British gold and arms was in reality something which it is very difficult to buy—viz., friendship. We wanted—it may safely be stated that we still want —a friendly Power to be established in Afghanistan. We had spent seventeen millions of English money and sacrificed many thousands of English and Indian lives, in the endeavour to make for ourselves a King of the Afghans who should be to our liking, and whom a sense of eternal gratitude for the recovery of his crown would bind to us completely. We had failed miserably. The very King we had made turned to plotting against us; the people rose, and with one great effort swept away our legions, burying them in the dark defiles of their mountains. The man we had hunted from his throne, and imprisoned for no fault, but because it suited the policy of the Government of the day to do so, had regained his throne in spite of us, and we expected to make him our very good friend by a payment of money. And for a time this mode of securing the friendship of the Afghan King succeeded, or at least appeared to succeed. Whether we are now, in the time of his successor, about to reap the fruits of this subsidising policy, the effect of which has been to strengthen a traditional enemy, to stiffen his neck with pride, and, perhaps, instil into him the notion that, after all, we have something to fear from his wrath, we leave to others to decide. In all £260,000 was paid to the then Amir of Cabul during the years 1856-58, the subsidy being continued for fourteen months after the war with Persia had ceased. The chief reason for the continuance of the subsidy scarcely needs to be stated. We were locked in a death-struggle with our own mutinous Indian army, and it was of the utmost importance that Dost Muhammad should refrain from attacking us, and should restrain his fierce subjects from a general Afghan invasion of the Panjab. And so Dost Muhammad—our former prisoner, whom we had so shabbily treated in 1838-40 —was now courted by an English Envoy, and his neutrality purchased at the price above mentioned. The spectacle was one not very creditable, perhaps, to a dignified Government; and no wonder Anglo-Indians have felt sore about it, and made apologies, on the ground of necessity and expediency, such as that above quoted. Unfortunately this was not the last occasion on which an Afghan Prince received English arms and gold in the vain effort to keep him "friendly." A time came—not long ago—when in haughty disdain Shere Ali flung back the proffered rupees, and has bided his time to avow the hostility that has all along only been latent. Barbarous nations delight in blood-feuds; and if ever there were grounds for a blood-feud between two nations, they exist in the case of the Afghans and ourselves.

It is the duty, however, of a nation calling itself civilised, not to say Christian, to restrain to the utmost those savage instincts which, in the case of individuals, are readily condemned, but in the case of nations are too often unchecked, if not actually fostered, by false ideas of patriotism.

Before passing on to more recent events, we should not omit to mention that Sir John (now Lord) Lawrence, on behalf of the Indian Government, signed a treaty in 1855 with the Amir Dost Muhammad Khan, in which we agreed to respect the territories of the Amir and his heirs, and the Amir, for himself and his heirs, agreed to respect the territories then in the possession of the East India Company, which have since devolved upon the Crown. Mr. Henry Richard, M.P., in some letters published recently in the *Christian World*, draws especial attention to this treaty in connection with the proposed "rectification" of our frontier. The only defence, we think, of which an infringement by us of the second article of this short treaty is at all capable is, that this second article may be held to have been cancelled by Shere Ali's violation of the first article, which declares that there shall be peace and *friendship* between the parties and their heirs. Shere Ali has apparently given his friendship to Russia. In January, 1857, Sir John Lawrence made a second agreement with Dost Muhammad, under which the latter received the subsidy of £10,000 per mensem (in addition to a previous present of £50,000), to which reference has already been made. For many years after his restoration Dost Muhammad's possessions were much curtailed, when compared with those that formerly owned the sway of the Durani monarchs before Shah Suja. Shah Suja himself had grumbled greatly when we replaced him on his throne at the diminished area of his kingdom, from which Herat, Cashmere, Peshawar, and Sindh had been lopped off. Dost Muhammad had little beyond the Cabul valley in his possession. His brothers at Candahar, and his nephew at Herat, were independent of him. When Kohandil Khan, of Candahar, however, died, Dost Muhammad overran the Western Afghan province, and soon afterwards commenced a contest with his nephew, Sultan Ahmad, for the possession of Herat. Persia naturally resented this attack on her virtual dependent, and we remonstrated with Dost Muhammad. He persevered, however, in his designs, and the climax was reached in the summer of 1863, without our having interfered further in the affair—by a triple and simultaneous catastrophe, the death of Sultan Ahmad by apoplexy, the fall of Herat to the Cabul army, and the crowning misfortune of the death of Dost Muhammad himself.

On the death of the great Barakzai chief, who had passed through so many vicissitudes of fortune, and whose name will go down to future generations, coupled with the history of the most calamitous period in our own history, Afghanistan relapsed into temporary anarchy amid the struggles that ensued for the succession. Dost Muhammad had nominated Shere Ali, a younger son by a favourite wife, to succeed him, passing over his many other sons, of whom Muhammad Afzal and Muhammad Azim, by an elder wife, were the most notable. Four pretenders in different parts of the country collected followers with a view to asserting their claims to the " masnad," or, as we should say, "throne ;" but the present rulers of Afghanistan avoid the title of " Shah " or King. Shere Ali for a short time made his authority recognised, but alienated many of the chiefs by placing one of his youngest sons, a youth of sixteen, named Yakub Khan, in the governorship of Herat. The standard of revolt was raised all over the country at almost the same moment, and Shere Ali was compelled to bend to the storm. His elder brother, Afzal Khan, succeeded in getting possession of Cabul, and was there proclaimed Amir of

Afghanistan, although Herat still held out against him for some time under Yakub Khan, who showed himself even at that youthful age, a leader of no mean capacity. He had indeed discovered a conspiracy in the interests of one of his uncles in Herat itself, and had suppressed it with firmness and complete success.

A few months after Shere Ali's defeat, which happened in 1866, Yakub was obliged to seek safety in flight, and Herat was captured by Afzal Khan. Yakub and his father became exiles, and the former ineffectually endeavoured to obtain assistance from the Persians. As they declined, however, to take part with Shere Ali, Yakub, nothing daunted by the failure of his negotiations, collected a small band of followers, and, after several smaller engagements round Herat, took that place by a vigorous attack at the head of 5,000 men. Many were attracted by Yakub's gallant achievements to his father's standard, and in 1868 he regained Candahar. Later on he rendered material assistance in the recapture of Cabul, when Shere Ali succeeded in driving out Azim, who had seized the Government on Afzal's death, in October, 1867. It was in September, 1868, that Shere Ali regained the throne, and it was almost directly afterwards that the famous quarrel broke out between him and his brave son, Yakub Khan, to whose valiant arm it may be said he owed his restoration. The Amir appears to have become suspicious of his son, fearing probably that his military capacity and reputation might render him a dangerous rival. At the same time Yakub discovered that Abdulla Jan's mother was intriguing to secure the succession to her son, a boy of tender years, but whose place in his father's regard was shown by his appointment to the Governorship of Candahar. Accordingly Yakub also resorted to intrigue with the view of keeping his hold upon Herat as governor, and at the same time he demanded to be recognised as Wali-Ahad or Heir-apparent. Shere Ali gave him no direct answer, and Yakub followed up his demand by others more sweeping, most of them relating to an enlarged share in the administration of the country. His father temporised by making partial concessions, which gave Yakub a voice in the government of the capital, but at the same time he surrounded him with adherents of his favourite son, the boy Abdulla Jan. Under these circumstances the position of the bold and ambitious Yakub became untenable. He perceived that nothing would prevent Abdulla Jan's nomination as heir-apparent; and in 1870 he fled from Cabul, accompanied by his full brother Ayub, a boy of thirteen or fourteen years. Yakub tried hard to provoke a rebellion against his father, but Shere Ali's influence had now become too strong for all that his sons could do against it. Yakub and his few adherents were beaten off from Candahar, Ghazni, and Girishk, and once more he took refuge in Persia. In the spring of 1871—this time with some Persian assistance—Yakub again laid siege to Herat, and it fell into his hands. Through the influence of Lord Mayo, father and son became reconciled. Yakub presented himself at Cabul and declared himself penitent; and in September of 1871 he was made Governor of Herat, but with a strong body of Shere Ali's adherents around him. Yakub and Shere Ali's nominees were never in accord, Yakub endeavouring to keep them from any real share in the administration, and they reporting to Cabul everything that might turn to Yakub's disadvantage. There can be little doubt that Yakub justified their reports, especially after the formal nomination of Abdulla Jan as heir-apparent in 1873. He intrigued with the Persians and the Turkomans; and it is believed that he also asked help of the Russians to assist him against his father; but he failed all round. The Amir declined his request to hold the governorship of Herat in perpetuity, free from Cabul influence, and in the autumn of 1874 summoned him to Cabul. Yakub suspected treachery, and demanded a safe conduct, which was granted. No sooner, however, had the young man arrived in the capital than his father put him under arrest, and he has been in confinement ever since. The Indian Government interceded with the Amir to spare his life, and to treat him well; but the first request only was granted. Yakub's imprisonment has been, according to the best accounts, very rigorous; and the story has filtered from Cabul into India that his intellect has been seriously affected by the harshness of his treatment. Yakub was a man of rare energy and talent, but he suffered from the disadvantage of having a mother of low birth—a circumstance which will seriously affect his chances of coming to the throne, if even it be untrue that he is insane, and supposing it possible for Shere Ali to become reconciled to him. Captain Marsh's interview with Yakub at Herat in 1873 revealed a not unfriendly disposition on Yakub's part towards England, and the traveller discovered that Yakub was one of the few Afghans who could speak English.

We may here shortly notice the other sons and nephews of Shere Ali, of whom, probably, one will have to be nominated to succeed the deceased youth, Abdulla Jan, as heir-apparent.

Ayub Khan, the full brother of Yakub, took no part in public affairs till he fled with Yakub from Cabul in 1870. The two lived together at Herat till Yakub set out on his hapless journey to Shere Ali in 1874; and when Ayub heard of his brother's arrest, he endeavoured to prepare Herat for resistance against his father, and to foment a rebellion in the neighbourhood, a project which failed. A few months afterwards he fled into Persian territory, where, meeting one of the Afghan generals who had been treacherous to Yakub's cause, he endeavoured to put him to death. The Persians prevented this. With Yakub's example before him, Ayub declined Shere Ali's invitation to return to Cabul, and we believe that Ayub has ever since lived in exile. He married a daughter of Shere Ali's half-brother Aslam, for whose murder Shere Ali was mainly responsible.

Another claimant to the throne of Cabul is Abdul Rahman, the son of Shere Ali's eldest brother Afzal. Rahman took a very active part in his father's cause against Shere Ali, and in the earlier stages of the war between Shere Ali and his brothers, he displayed as much military skill as his cousin Yakub. In the end, however, Shere Ali defeated him, and he took refuge at Tashkend. For the past five years the Russians have given this man £3,000 a year as a subsidy, so that they may have a nominee of their own at hand if disputes again arise in the Afghan succession. Abdul Rahman has been to St. Petersburg; he is thoroughly Russianised, is considered a very able man, and Shere Ali is said to be greatly in fear of his influence in the district of Balkh.

In addition to these three, Yakub, Ayub, and

Abdul Rahman, there is another aspirant to the throne who does not lie under the disadvantage of having incurred the Amir's hostility. This is Ahmad Ali, a youth of seventeen, the son of Shere Ali's eldest son, who fell in battle at the head of his father's army, in 1865, in a hand-to-hand encounter with his father's uncle, who was also left dead on the field. This young man has always been in favour with the Amir, and would probably have been proclaimed heir-apparent instead of the late Abdulla Jan but for the influence of the mother of that prince. He is now considered to have the best chance of being nominated as Shere Ali's successor, Abdulla Jan having died quite recently, since, indeed, the project of an English Mission to Cabul was announced.

Abdul Rahman's only hope is in Russian influence. Even if Yakub be released, and found in full possession of his faculties after his long and severe imprisonment, it is doubtful whether the Afghan nobles would give him much cordial support, as his low birth on his mother's side stands in the way of his popularity with the haughty Afghan chiefs. He is by the latest accounts, however, still in prison. It is considered unlikely that the English Government would heartily support Yakub, because he is believed to have intrigued with Russia during his latter days at Herat. We have continued our account of the domestic affairs of Afghanistan down to the present time.

There is much of importance still to be said of the foreign relations of the Amir towards Russia and England, and these will be considered in the next and concluding chapters.

CHAPTER IX.

RUSSIAN ADVANCE EASTWARDS.

Chief Difficulty in Understanding the Central Asian Question—Importance of the News of the Arrival of a Russian Mission at Cabul—Its Mention in Parliament—Treatment of the Russian Mission—Reason of Importance Attached to Independence of Afghanistan—Excessive Cost of Present Indian Forces of Great Britain—Our Real Concern with Afghanistan—Two Schools of Opinion on our Indian Frontier Policy—Lord Beaconsfield's Definition of " The Afghan Question "—His Enunciation of England's Present Policy—Review of Negotiations with the Amir—Dost Muhammad's Virtue in Abstaining from Revenge in 1857—Lord Lawrence's so-called " Masterly Inactivity "—Succeeded by Different Policy of " Mischievous Activity "—Recognition of Shere Ali—The Amballa Meeting between Lord Mayo and Shere Ali—Lord Mayo's Declaration to the Amir Examined—Practical Assistance in Money and Arms to Shere Ali—Shere Ali's Oversanguine Expectations—View taken of Lord Mayo's Proceedings by Home Government—Lord Mayo's Explanation—Correspondence Concerning a " Neutral Zone "—How " Neutral Zone " Defined in 1872—Russian Expedition to Khiva—Its Importance to India—The Worth of Russian Assurances—Lord Granville's Remonstrances—Expedition against the Turkomans—Shere Ali's Alarm at Russia's Advance—Sends his Confidential Agent to Simla—His Proposals to Lord Northbrook—Failure of Negotiations—Shere Ali Communicates with General Kauffmann—Further Russian Official Assurances—So-called Exploring Expedition in 1875—Expedition against Kizil Arvat in 1876—Russian Advance in Bokhara and Khokand—Choice of Three Routes for Russian Advance on Afghan Frontier—Projected Railways—Russian Activity in Central Asia in Spring of 1878—Last Reported Russian Assurance—Latest Advance towards India.

IN the last chapter we completed the outline of Afghan history up to the present time, reserving

Shere Ali's relations with his Russian and English neighbours for consideration along with the wider subject of what is called the Central Asian question. Sir Henry Rawlinson and other able men have for years been labouring to render this difficult subject intelligible to the English reader. There is naturally a fascination about it for Anglo-Indians which leads them on through long and too often dreary pages crammed full of Oriental names of men and places dressed in such fantastic guises that they become frequently insoluble puzzles to those who are versed in Oriental languages, and must be the most hopeless enigmas to the ordinary English reader.

The extremely technical nature of most discourses on the Central Asian question has probably had much to do with the indifference with which the English people have treated it. They cannot be expected to care much about matters which even experts do not always seem to understand, and so the news from India that a new page in the history of Afghan foreign politics had been opened excited about as much general interest as if it had been announced that the Sultan of Turkey had been deposed and another appointed in his place.

Those, however, who called to mind that the presence of a Russian agent (Viktevitch) at Cabul had been one of the proximate causes of our interference in Afghan politics in 1838, and of our subsequent disasters, attached more importance to the news that General Abramoff had been sent to Cabul by General Kauffmann, at present Russian Governor-General of Tashkend, but better known perhaps as the successful commander in the expedition against Khiva. We have since learnt that the officer sent in charge of this so-called " commercial " mission was General Stolieteff, not Abramoff. We naturally credited the Russians with as much honesty in styling their mission a " commercial " one as we ourselves exercised when we sent Captain (afterwards Sir Alexander) Burnes, in 1837, to Dost Muhammad's Court with a view to gaining him over as an ally against Russo-Persian aggression. We called Burnes's mission "commercial," although it was political from the first, and had an object very far from friendly to Russia. *Ergo*, we supposed Russia meant General Stolieteff to exercise other than mere " commercial " functions at Cabul. The closing hours of the last Session of Parliament were harassed by questions from anxious members as to the truth of reports from India which spoke of the projected despatch of an English mission to Cabul to counteract the influence of the Russian envoy. The news of the latter's arrival at Cabul reached us on the 11th of August. We heard at the same time that Lord Lytton had, on the 22nd July preceding that, addressed letters to the Amir. The Russian mission, we now know, had reached Cabul in June, after (it is alleged) Shere Ali had shown great disinclination to receive it. Once, however, in his capital, he appears to have treated his unbidden guests well, to have given them a royal salute, to have held a review of his troops in their honour, and to have sent a mission of his own to General Kauffmann in return. Part of the Russian mission remained behind at Cabul, and the rest returned to Tashkend with the Afghan officers of the Amir. We have heard plenty of rumours since of caravans of Russian arms and ammunition having reached Cabul, and of Russian officers swarming into Afghanistan to drill the Afghan troops after the most approved European methods.

Of what has actually passed between the Amir and his Russian visitors we *know* hardly anything, and we can only conjecture from his conduct since their arrival whether he has given ear to their counsels or not.

The reader will scarcely now need to be told that for years past it has been an axiom with most Anglo-Indian politicians that any interference by Russia with Afghanistan ought to be made a subject of remonstrance and, if necessary, of war. The reason for this state of feeling has been obviously the dread that if Russia were permitted to establish herself in Afghanistan, she would thereby be enabled to consolidate her power in Central Asia, to complete her long line of communication with her European provinces, not only through the difficult tracts of desert and steppe that now separate Orenburgh from Tashkend, but through the territories of Persia, over which Alexander the Great marched with so much apparent ease to India, and so threaten our Indian frontier in a way that can hardly now be realised. The consequence of Russia's possession of Afghanistan would, it is believed, be to put British India in perpetual dread of Russian invasion; and as our Indian feudatories and fellow-subjects are supposed to be particularly sensitive to Russophobia, and many of them, indeed, have been even credited with a willingness to get rid of our yoke altogether at the risk of only changing their masters, the one certain result of such an event would be that a large army of observation would be required to guard our existing frontier. Those who think we are not justified in extending our frontier, even by peaceful negotiation —believing that a still more advanced frontier would be still more costly to defend—do not deny that if Russian influence were to become paramount in Afghanistan, we should have to keep up a larger European army than at present in India.

Few persons are aware how large a proportion of the revenues of India are already expended for military purposes. The Indian army charges for the current year are estimated at £15,800,000, while the whole revenue derived from Excise, Customs, salt duties, stamps, and land revenue, is rather less than £35,000,000. We thus see that in India nearly one-half of the taxes are spent for military purposes; while in England, which is as rich as India is poor, the army expenses for the current year are estimated at £15,595,800, or less than one-fourth of the revenue derived from Customs, Excise, stamps, land tax, income tax, and house duty, which amounts to about £66,500,000. Again, if the results of the army expenditure in England and India are compared, it will be seen that while the expenditure for both services is almost identical, the strength of the English service is—regular army, 128,037; army reserve (first and second class), 43,000; militia and militia reserve, 136,778; and volunteers and yeomanry, 254,734—or a total of 562,549 men. On the other hand, the Indian army numbers only 62,650 European and 125,000 native troops, or a total of about 188,000 men. The excessive cost of the Indian army—two-thirds of which is composed of native forces—as compared with that of England, seems to demand attention, with a view to a decrease, if possible, rather than an augmentation.

Thus, if we once grant the assumption that Russia intends, if left alone, to advance her frontier practically to the Suliman Mountains and the Khaibar Pass, we cannot avoid the conclusion that such a proceeding on her part will involve us in heavy expenditure.

If our present frontier were universally considered defensible, no one could reasonably hope to persuade England to go to war with Russia in order to keep her out of Afghanistan. We do not ourselves want that country for its own sake; but the utmost concern we could feel with regard to it is that it should either be independent and friendly, or so under our control as to be prevented from being used against us by Russia.

Those who regard our present frontier as a sufficiently strong one, or as capable of being made so, or, at least, that it is better to put up with it than advance it any further, object with great vehemence to the recent policy of Lord Lytton and the Conservative Government as needlessly involving us in complications that may lead to a war which they think would have no adequate cause. To this school belong such high authorities as Lord Lawrence, General Sir John Adye, Lords Mayo, Northbrook, and Napier, and Sir Henry Norman. To these, Mr. Fawcett adds the Duke of Wellington, Lord Hardinge, Lord Sandhurst, Sir Herbert Edwardes, General Nicholson, General Beecher, and General Reynell Taylor. On the other side are ranged Sir Bartle Frere, the late Governor of Bombay, and, apparently, the present military advisers of Lord Lytton and the Premier.

We have spoken of "the Afghan question" hitherto as if it were merely one concerning the rectification of our Indian frontier. In doing so we have followed the line taken by Lord Beaconsfield in his speech at the Mansion House on November 9th. Our readers will remember that on that occasion the Premier said:—"So far as the invasion of India in that quarter [meaning on the north-western frontier] is concerned, it is the opinion of Her Majesty's Government that it is hardly practicable. The base of operations of any possible foe is so remote, the communications are so difficult, the aspect of the country so forbidding, that we have long arrived at an opinion that an invasion of our Empire by passing the mountains which form our north-western frontier is one which we need not dread. But it is a fact that that frontier is a haphazard, and not a scientific frontier; and it is possible that it is in the power of any foe so to embarrass and disturb our dominion that we should, under the circumstances, be obliged to maintain a great military force in that quarter, and, consequently, entail upon this country and upon India a greatly increased expenditure. These are evils not to be despised, and, as I venture to observe, they have for some time, under various Viceroys and under different Administrations, occupied the attention of our statesmen. But while our attention was naturally drawn also to this subject, some peculiar circumstances occurred in that part of the world which rendered it absolutely necessary that we should give our immediate and earnest attention to the subject, and see whether it was not possible to terminate that absolute inconvenience and possible injury, which must or would accrue if the present state of affairs were not touched and considered by the Government of the Queen. With these views we have taken such measures as we think will effect the object we require. When these arrangements are made—and I cannot suppose that any considerable time will elapse before they are consummated—our north-western frontier will no longer be a source of anxiety to the English people. We shall live, I hope, on good terms with our immediate neighbours, and perhaps not on bad terms with some neighbours that are more remote. But, in making these remarks I should be sorry for it to be believed that it was the opinion of Her Majesty's Government that an invasion of India was impossible or impracticable. On the contrary, if Asia Minor and the Valley of the Euphrates were in the possession of a very weak or of a very powerful State, an adequate force might march through the passes of the Asian mountains, through Persia, and absolutely menace the empire of the Queen. Well, we have foreseen that possibility, and have provided for what we believe will secure its non-occurrence, and the chief mode by which we have provided for that result is that convention with Turkey of which you have heard so much. By that convention we have secured that the regions in question shall be in the possession of an ally, and at the same time, if he fulfils, as we do not doubt he will fulfil, the conditions of that agreement, they will be in the possession of an ally supported by subjects whose prosperity every year will render his authority more firm and valid. In effecting this result we have occupied the island of Cyprus, in order to encourage and strengthen and aid the Sultan." We have quoted the whole passage referring to Afghan affairs, as it contained the most authoritative statement we had had given to us up to that date of the state of our relations with the Amir. It was an important disclosure which informed us that "the Afghan question" was one mainly of "a rectification of frontier," and not, as the English public for some time believed, a question of upholding the honour of England against insult.

Without discussing further here the merits and demerits of the rival frontier policies, we continue our brief review of the negotiations that have passed between the Indian Government and the Amir of Afghanistan since the death of Dost Muhammad in 1863. It will be remembered that we had concluded a treaty with Dost Muhammad in 1855, by which each party bound himself to respect the integrity of the other's territories, a treaty which was followed by a subsidy of £10,000 a month during our war with Persia, and until we put down the Indian mutiny. The virtue displayed by Dost Muhammad in abstaining from an invasion of Northern India during the mutiny of 1857 has been so loudly extolled of late that it is desirable to point out to those who would attribute it to excessive generosity on his part that there were two very good reasons why he did not avail himself of the opportunity to strike a blow against us : first, that he was paid handsomely not to do so ; and secondly, that he had seen with what ease the English had dethroned him in 1839, and how effectually we had avenged our subsequent disasters. Lord Northbrook has especially referred to Dost Muhammad's forbearance as proof of the good results of conciliation. This latter reflection may have had quite as much to do with keeping him staunch as any feeling of generosity, a sentiment which he could hardly be expected to entertain towards the British Power.

From the death of Dost Muhammad to the year 1868 Afghanistan was the scene of internecine wars, a short summary of which has been given in the last chapter. Lord Lawrence was Governor-General during that period, and as one of his successors in the Viceroyalty (Lord Northbrook) said of his policy the other day, " most wisely abstained from all interference" in these domestic quarrels, "only saying that whoever became ruler of the country would be recognised as such by the British Government." It was to this abstention on the part of Lord Lawrence from interference in the affairs of Afghanistan that the late Mr. Wyllie, an Indian civilian whom Lord Northbrook described as "very able," applied the term "masterly inactivity," of which so much has been made since. The phrase, however, of masterly inactivity in no way applied to the policy pursued since that day. Indeed, Mr. Wyllie himself, who had written the article headed "Masterly Inactivity" in the *Fortnightly Review*, wrote another called "Mischievous Activity," and gave the reasons he had to advance against the policy afterwards pursued by Lords Lawrence and Mayo after the civil war in Afghanistan had come to an end. This later policy consisted in extending to Shere Ali, who had got the upper hand of his brothers, that moral support which had been previously withheld, and of entering into closer relations with him. With regard to both these lines of policy Lord Northbrook has recently given his opinion that they were wisely adopted. When the resolve to recognise Shere Ali was made, Lord Beaconsfield was Premier and Sir Stafford Northcote Secretary of State for India. Lord Lawrence, however, resigned office to Lord Mayo in January, 1869, before the new programme had been carried out. We know that it included one of those gorgeous State ceremonies in which the Orientals and Conservative Premiers are said to delight. Lord Mayo met Shere Ali at Amballa in March, and had a conference with him, surrounded by all the pomp which attends those viceregal assemblies, and, after hearing all that Shere Ali wanted, he decided what he would give him, and what he did not feel it consistent with British interests to give him, and, as Lord Mayo has been challenged a good deal by the Press as to what he did, it is only fair to him to use his own words as to what he intended to give and what he did give on that occasion. He said on the 1st of July, 1869:—"While we distinctly intimated to the Amir that under no circumstances should a British soldier ever cross his frontier to assist him in coercing his rebellious subjects; that no European officers should be placed as residents in his cities; that no fixed subsidy or money allowance should be given for any named period; that no promises of assistance in other ways should be made; that no treaty would be entered into obliging us under any circumstances to recognise him and his descendants as rulers in Afghanistan, we were prepared by the most open and absolute present recognition, and by every public evidence of friendly disposition, of respect for his character, and interest in his fortunes, to give all the moral support in our power, and, in addition, we were willing to assist him with money, arms, ammunition, and native artificers, and in other ways, whenever we deem it possible or desirable to do so."

Three matters in this declaration specially deserve notice. First, Lord Mayo promised that no European officer should be placed in Shere Ali's territory without his consent. This was only following the request of Dost Muhammad, who had said, in 1856, to Lord Lawrence, "If we are to be friends, do not force British officers upon me." The sound policy of this promise, which seemed like a concession, has been questioned, but a later Viceroy has approved of it, for the apparently very good reason that "unless British officers were to be there on good relations, they would be of no use whatever." It must not be supposed either, that because we were not to have European officers accredited to Shere Ali's Court, the Viceroy would be unrepresented. A native Envoy has, until the present rupture in our relations with him, uninterruptedly resided at the Amir's Court.

The second matter to be observed is the rejection of a proposal for a treaty guaranteeing his dominions unconditionally from without.

The third point is the refusal of a promise to support any one at his death whom he might have nominated heir. To have guaranteed his dominions unconditionally would have been to encourage him to attack his neighbours; and to have given the promise to support his nominee in obtaining the "masnad" after his death would have been to commit ourselves to interfere in the domestic policy of Afghanistan, and against such interference we had had sufficient warning in former years.

To counter-balance our refusal of these requests "practical assistance in the shape of money and war materials" was offered to the extent of 12 lakhs of rupees (£1,200,000) in all, besides arms, guns, and ammunition. The only return which the Governor-General expected for this being "abiding confidence, sincerity, and goodwill."

Sir Henry Rawlinson remarks upon this transaction, that Lord Clarendon may have been "justified —in so far as he possessed any knowledge of the intentions of the Indian Government—in assuring Prince Gortschakoff at Heidelberg that Sir John Lawrence's policy in assisting Shere Ali Khan 'had no reference to the advances of Russia in Central Asia;' but no one conversant with the negotiations which preceded the Amballa Conference can doubt that these advances did exercise a very important influence on the feelings and conduct of the Amir of Cabul."

But, however clear and unqualified the refusal of Lord Mayo to the proposed guarantee and promise of future support may appear to us now, it is not certain that, in 1869, Shere Ali did not believe he had been granted more than in fact was conceded. For Lord Mayo did give a written declaration that the British Government "would view with severe displeasure any attempt on the part of his rivals to disturb his position." Coupling this with Sir John Lawrence's promise of "practical assistance in the shape of money and materials of war," to be furnished to him in the future "at the discretion of the head of the administration in India," and Lord Mayo's confirmatory declarations that "any representation he might make would always be treated with consideration and respect," it is believed Shere Ali went away understanding these expressions of general interest in a more liberal sense than they were meant to convey. It is thought, says Sir Henry Rawlinson, that he considered "the threat of 'severe displeasure' to be equivalent to an assurance of armed support against his allies, while the promised consideration of his future demands amounted in his view, to an almost unlimited credit on the Indian Exchequer."

Two views of Lord Mayo's proceedings were taken by the authorities in England. The bolder spirits would have preferred a bolder policy, to the extent of accepting the liability of an armed intervention by giving the Amir a direct guarantee of protection against insurrection and also invasion, taking due advantage of the favourable positions we should then have obtained to secure the Afghan frontiers, and to establish our influence permanently in the country. The more cautious statesmen with whom the decision rested were, on the contrary, of opinion that Lord Mayo had already gone too far, the threat of "severe displeasure" against Shere Ali's internal enemies having probably committed us to a more active interference in Afghan politics than had been contemplated, or suited the interests of India.

Lord Mayo explained that, without risking the failure of the whole scheme, he could not avoid using the language objected to, and pointed to the results, in Shere Ali's strengthened position at Cabul, as the best justification of his policy.

On the very day of the Umballa Conference a very important correspondence on Central Asian affairs was commenced between Lord Clarendon, the British Foreign Minister, and the Russian Government. This had for its object the demarcation of what has been called "a neutral zone" of territory between the frontier of undoubted British and Russian dominions. The suggestions for laying down such a zone sprang from the anxiety to allay the increasing disquietude of the Native States along the north-west frontier of India, which was caused by the persistent approaches of Russia. The Government of Lord Mayo regarded the proposal almost as an attack on their independent action; but Lord Clarendon seems to have really thought it desirable in the interests of both Governments to have a neutral zone. The great objection to such an arrangement would be that it would make either Power responsible to the other for its dealings with the peoples inhabiting their frontiers, many of whom often require chastisement for marauding attacks on the subjects of the great Powers. The correspondence dragged its slow length along, characterised by some geographical errors not creditable to our Foreign Office, until 1872, when Her Majesty's Government notified to Russia the extent of territory which Shere Ali claimed on the Upper Oxus, and to which they were prepared to recognise his right. In expressing the boundaries native authority had to be followed, for we knew little or nothing of the bend of the river Oxus to the northward, or of the upper feeders from Pamir. Thus it was not defined which of the feeders was the main stream of the Oxus, and so for a time it seemed that part of Wakhan had been abandoned to Russia. Subsequent inquiries seem to show that the feeder entitled to be considered the main stream really forms the northern boundary of that province. The territories thus indicated as belonging to Afghanistan were then formally declared by Prince Gortchakoff to be "completely outside the sphere within which Russia might be called to exercise her influence." The Russian boundary line is therefore that of her dependencies, Khokand and Bokhara, and is conterminous with the frontiers of Badakhshan and Wakhan, which were conceded by Russia to belong to the Amir. We may here briefly refer to the Russian conquest of Khiva in 1873. This expedition, says Rawlinson, "affords an apt illustration of the normal course of Russian progress in the East." It resulted in the annexation of a large extent of territory to the Russian Empire, and reduced Khiva to a perfect state of vassalage, and thus finally secured access to those strategic lines across the Steppe, which were essential to Russia's further progress, and which had been, in fact, the primary object of the expedition.

But the importance to India of the Khivan campaign, and its results, perhaps, chiefly lies in the remarkable light thrown by them upon Russian diplomacy. More notable instances of repudiation of promises could scarcely be found in modern history than those given by Prince Gortchakoff in the course of the representations that passed between him and the British Foreign Office.

Khiva had been mentioned during the earlier

negotiations in 1869 that aimed at making the Oxus the limit of Russian influence. The Russian Ambassador in London had objected to that river being the boundary, because it would include a portion of Khiva which lies to the south of the Oxus, and Russia would then be debarred from punishing the ruler for outrages on Russian subjects. Lord Clarendon, the English Foreign Minister, admitted the right of the Czar to punish the Khan "on his own territory," but added this important proviso :—" That England would rely on the honour of Russia, as soon as she had obtained reparation, again to revert to the arrangement, should she have assented to it, and consider the Upper Oxus as the boundary which was not to be passed." Shortly after that conversation rumours of an intended expedition against Khiva assumed a definite shape, and Sir A. Buchanan, our Ambassador at St. Petersburg, questioned Prince Gortchakoff on the subject. The Chancellor denied that the Russian Government had any intention " to despatch a military expedition to Khiva." He declared, moreover, that " he would never consent to any further extension of the territory of the empire." " Prince Gortchakoff's language was so apparently sincere," exclaimed Sir A. Buchanan, " that, notwithstanding the strong grounds which exist for believing that an expedition is preparing against Khiva, I shall endeavour " to believe every word the

Russian Chancellor has said. In the course of some further conversation on the Khivan question in June, 1870, Prince Gortchakoff assured the English Ambassador that "Russia neither required nor desired to possess the khanates." Khokand and Bokhara, he said, were ready to act according to her wishes, but Khiva was still disposed to be hostile. Nevertheless, at the same moment, Russia was secretly preparing an expedition to Khiva; while as to Bokhara, within two months of the last-mentioned date Russia took the important Bokharian fortress of Shahr-i-subz (August 24, 1870). But the promises about Khiva still went on.

In June, 1871, it was admitted that an expedition to punish the Khan of Khiva for attacks on caravans had been thought of, but we were assured that it would not take place. In March, 1872, the Director of the Asiatic Department at St. Petersburg (M. Stremooukoff) admitted that reconnaissances had been already made against Khiva, and that the Russian generals had found "the occupation of the place would offer no strategical difficulties." In summing up the result of his conversation with M. Stremooukoff, Lord Augustus Loftus wrote:—" I have gained the conviction that an expedition against Khiva is decided upon, and will be made as soon as the weather and circumstances permit." Six or seven months later the Russian papers announced that the expedition had been prepared, but M. Westmann denied (in September) that measures had advanced to such a stage. He, however, practically admitted that if the Khan interfered with commerce, and refused to give up the Russian prisoners, the Russian Government would punish him. As the winter advanced evidence increased of the Russian intention to send a force against Khiva. The subject came up, as we have already described, in the celebrated interview between Count Schouvaloff and Lord Granville. The Russian representative admitted that an expedition was decided upon for the spring, but declared that both its composition and its objects would be insignificant. The force would consist of "but four-and-a-half battalions," and its objects would be "to punish acts of brigandage, to recover fifty Russian prisoners, and to teach the Khan that such conduct on his part could not be continued. Not only," continued Count Schouvaloff, "was it far from the intention of the Emperor to take possession of Khiva, but positive orders had been prepared to prevent it, and directions given that the conditions imposed should be such as could not in any way lead to a prolonged occupancy of Khiva." It was not long before the departure of the expedition gave an opportunity for testing the veracity of one of Count Schouvaloff's promises. The insignificant force of four-and-a-half battalions grew into three columns, which altogether numbered about 10,000 men, and was accompanied by forty guns. On June 10, 1873, Khiva fell, and the time came for fulfilling the second of Count Schouvaloff's engagements. The treaty which was imposed upon the Khan, in face of the Russian promise to make no territorial accessions, bestowed on Russia the whole of the Khivan territory on the right bank of the Oxus. Besides thus taking possession of a large extent of country, the treaty prepared the way for the entire absorption of the khanate, if Russia were so minded. It imposed an enormous indemnity, the payment of which extended over nineteen years ; it extorted a declaration from the Khan of Russian suzerainty, and a renunciation of the right to maintain diplomatic relations or enter into treaties with the rulers of neighbouring khanates. Russia also obtained exclusive control of the navigation of the Oxus, and the right to establish commercial buildings on the left bank of the river.

Lord Granville, when the treaty was communicated to him in January, 1874, merely replied, in cold and measured terms, that " Her Majesty's Government saw no practical advantage in examining too minutely how far the Khivan arrangements were in strict accordance with the assurances given by Count Schouvaloff as to the intentions with which the expedition was undertaken." " This dignified rebuke," says Sir Henry Rawlinson, "seems to have rankled somewhat in the hearts of the Russian statesmen, who, however, did not condescend to any apology or explanation further than by calling their acquisition of territory on the right bank of the Oxus 'sterile and onerous,' and contrasting its disadvantages with the brilliant position they might have gained had they yielded to the pressing invitation of the Khan that they should place a garrison in the town of Khiva." Lord Granville, however, proposed another arrangement. He declared the necessity of "a clear and frank understanding" as to the relative position of British and Russian interests in Asia, but suggested no definite plan for the attainment of that object further than to recommend another pledge from Russia not to take Merv nor interfere with the independence of the Amir of Afghanistan. Lord Granville's moderation proved very agreeable to the Government of St. Petersburg. Prince Gortchakoff expressed his "entire satisfaction" at the "just view which Lord Granville had taken." "In my opinion," he exclaimed, "the understanding is complete." All that was required, according to his opinion, for the future agreement of the two Governments was a spirit of mutual goodwill and conciliation. The understanding between the two Powers rested "not only upon the loyalty of the two Governments, but upon mutual political advantages." As a proof of this loyalty, he repeated "the positive assurance that the Imperial Cabinet continues to consider Afghanistan as entirely beyond its sphere of action." This was in January, 1874.

It is necessary here to follow in some detail the advances of Russia in Central Asia since the fall of Khiva. The most important event, perhaps, in her progress eastwards has been the subjugation of the Yomút and Goklan Turkomans. This has pushed her frontier on towards Merv, a large city and a strong strategical position, which was supposed to be her next object. Shere Ali, alarmed at the reported advance upon Merv, as well as by the example of the Khivan Expedition, had sent his confidential agent in September, 1873, to wait on the Viceroy (Lord Northbrook) at Simla to discuss the general question of the Indo-Afghan relations.

In those negotiations it is curious to observe that the Amir treated the safety of Afghanistan as essentially necessary to the safety of India, and he proposed that the British Government should assist him with money and arms. Money he had already received to the extent of two lakhs of rupees, and he was now promised ten lakhs in addition, as well as 10,000 Enfield and 5,000 Snider rifles. But it soon appeared that these large grants did not satisfy the Amir's wants. He evidently thought it the duty of England to supply him with whatever he deemed necessary to make Afghanistan secure from invasion. He dreaded a Russian advance upon Merv, and he wished to make this country responsible for protecting him against the consequences of that advance being continued to Herat. The English Government showed no unwillingness to accept a considerable share of the duty which the Afghan ruler desired to place upon them. It was declared that "in the event of any aggression from without, the British Government would in all probability afford material assistance in repelling an invader," and Lord Derby stated in the House of Lords (May 8, 1874) that "it was highly probable this country would interfere" in the case of any attack upon the independence of Afghanistan. Nevertheless, the negotiations with the Amir did not progress favourably. The chief obstacle to a definite course of action arose from the refusal of Shere Ali to enter into reciprocal engagements. He declined to accept a proposed survey by English officers of the frontier which he considered to be exposed to Russian attack; and he was equally indisposed to permit the presence of Residents at Cabul, Herat, or Candahar, whom the English Government desired to place there in order to prevent this country from undertaking any measures on behalf of Shere Ali without knowing why. From that period we may date the defection of Shere Ali from the English alliance. Shortly after the Simla conference had revealed to the Amir that England considered some return for her responsibility necessary on his part, we find him in communication with General Kaufmann. That officer was wise enough to express horror at the rebellion of Yakub Khan, which naturally pleased the Amir better than our intercession in the young Prince's behalf. But all the time that General Kaufmann was thus coquetting with Shere Ali, Prince Gortchakoff was renewing his promises to have nothing to do with Afghanistan.

For although the last official correspondence which the English Government has thought fit to publish dates as far back as January, 1874—when Prince Gortchakoff replied to Lord Granville's remonstrance about Khiva—we have gleaned from time to time through the Indian, German, and Russian Press some information as to the course of events.* " Thus in the summer of 1875, when it was supposed that a Russian expedition directed against the Turkomans would seize Kizil Arvat, as a step towards Merv, it was also declared by an Indian newspaper that Russia had pledged herself not to extend her territory in the direction of the Atrek river."†

* See Publishers' Note prefixed.
† Persia claimed that her territories extend beyond this river to its watershed, and include the valleys of all the

Within a few weeks of that engagement we had news of a scientific exploring expedition, starting from Krasnovodsk to "the old bed of the Oxus." Instead, however, of its having that innocent object, it turned out to be a Cossack force from Chikisliar, along the course of the Atrek, which succeeded in obtaining the submission of certain tribes in the neighbourhood of that river and the Simbar. This was in 1875, and other expeditions followed in 1876 and 1877. All this time the Russian Government, according to their semi-official journals, were endeavouring to restrict General Lomakin's operations, and it came with surprise upon this country in 1876 that in the course of that year a small Russian expedition had actually reached Kizil Arvat. That demonstration, however, seems to have been no more than a reconnaissance; but in the following year a new expedition, consisting of 4,000 men, marched in the same direction. Beyond the announcement that the force reached Kizil Arvat, the Russian newspapers threw no light upon its operations. Current reports, which were probably true, represented that General Lomakin suffered a severe defeat, and this was ultimately admitted by

affluents of that river, to the north of which the Simbar is one, and she also claimed the Yomuts inhabiting those valleys as her subjects. Little regard, however, has been paid by Russia to this claim, as she has established a military post on the Atrek.

the *Russki Mir*. The information supplied by the Indian Press respecting these expeditions indicates that the Russian endeavour to advance towards Merv was not overlooked by the Viceroy and his Council. These were the days of Lord Salisbury's appeals to large-scale maps, and he seems to have rejected all proposals that may have been made by the Indian Government for counteracting Russian enterprise against the Turkomans and Merv. It may be that the Indian Secretary received some assurances from the Russian authorities that Merv was not to be interfered with, and that his simple faith in Russia's promises was undisturbed. Indeed, an Allahabad paper recently announced that in 1876 Prince Gortchakoff added one more to the long series of pledges "to regard Afghanistan as remaining outside the sphere of Russia's action."

Meanwhile, Russia's advance was being continued in Bokhara and Khokand. Khokand had become Russian territory, and the last remnants of Bokhara's independence had been destroyed. Although the Czar and his Chancellor had professed to regret the conquest of the northern portion of Bokhara, and had even promised to restore Samarkand to the Amir of Bokhara, yet, in 1873, they compelled him to enter into a treaty, by which he virtually placed his country in the possession of Russia.

The course of procedure with regard to Khokand

was exactly similar. In that case also there were the professed regrets at the cruel necessity of annexing a portion of the territory. There were the same promises that the terms of Russian advance in that region had been reached, and that what was left should be independent. Nevertheless, on the 7th of February, 1876, the portion of the country that had been suffered to remain under the rule of Khudayar Khan was annexed, and received the name of Ferghana, its feudatory State of Karateghin being alone left in a condition of semi-independence.

Russia has thus, by means of her recent conquests, obtained the choice of three routes by which she can advance upon the Afghan frontier from the Oxus. These are—first, from Charjui through Merv to Herat; second, from Karshi to Andkhui; and, third, by Khoja Salih ferry to Balkh and the Bamian Pass. She would then have the Oxus, with its steamboat service to and from Lake Aral, for her base and source of supplies. It is certain, also, that she would be able to greatly strengthen her position in Turkestan in the course of a few years, if allowed to do so, by railways through Persia, connecting the Russian possessions on the Oxus directly with the ports of the Black Sea. There are several such schemes at present *in nubibus*, but capable of development, if opportunity offers. The most feasible of these seems to be the proposal to make a railway from Batoum on the Black Sea, which has now become a Russian port, to Erivan, Tabriz, and Teheran, thus passing through the eastern extremity of Armenia and the Persian provinces of Azerbijan, Ghilan, and Mazanderan. This would have to be continued through Khorasan for another seven or eight hundred miles, to connect Batoum with Herat.

The Russian system of railways ends at present at Orenburg, and no scheme of continuing it through Khiva to Merv has been suggested but may be regarded as purely imaginary. But the expectations that have been raised by mooting these schemes are altogether extravagant. Persia is miserably poor, and no railway such as the one suggested would pay. It is doubtful, too, whether Russia, after the late exhausting war, has any means of raising the enormous sums that such gigantic undertakings would require. Her hold on the newly-conquered provinces of Turkestan will require to be further strengthened, and her administration more fully organised, before such schemes will commend themselves to her own or foreign capitalists; even were she to attempt to raise the necessary funds by guaranteeing a remunerative rate of interest, after the example set by the Indian Government.

That she is disposed to be inactive in Central Asia is negatived by the recent events there. Long before the Congress met at Berlin, and while the question of peace or war between Russia and England seemed to be trembling in the balance, preparations, we now know, were being made to strike a blow, or, at least, to create a diversion, in the direction of India, England's most vulnerable quarter. No sensible person can blame Russia for taking such a step in what she may have fairly deemed to be her best interests, but nothing is surely gained by denying that she had, or could have, any hostile intentions towards England by any movements of troops in Asia. If, as is now fully believed, an expedition was being concentrated, as early as April, 1878, at Krasnovodsk, on the Caspian, with the ostensible object of attacking the Tekkeh Turkomans, and of seizing Merv, no one acquainted with the importance attached by the Indian Government to Merv as the last stage towards Herat, which is regarded as "the Gate of India," can wonder that this movement appeared to Anglo-Indian politicians as intended to be a demonstration against India. Kizil Arvat, which is the half-way house, so to speak, to Merv, has been captured; but we have no intelligence whether the Krasnovodsk column has advanced beyond that place. Some persons are assured that it returned immediately after the signature of the Berlin Treaty was known at St. Petersburg. Other reports state, however, that on the very day the Berlin Treaty was signed the

Russian envoy was directed to advance to Cabul, and that the Krasnovodsk column is still hovering about Merv.

Accurate information is still wanting as to the real movements of these troops, but it is stated that it was a part of the Russian plan that the Krasnovodsk column should act in co-operation with the army whose movements accompanied the progress of the Russian envoy to the Afghan capital. The Eastern Turkestan forces are said to have numbered about 15,000 men. There were three columns, but only one or two at the most reached the neighbourhood of the Upper Oxus. The *Turkestan Gazette* announced that Samarkand was to be the rendezvous of the principal column. The right wing was to concentrate at a fort opposite Khiva and march to Charjui, to operate, no doubt, with the Krasnovodsk column against Merv. The left wing was to be established in Ferghana. How far these three columns advanced southwards we have no intelligence. Three months ago the statement was current that the Ferghana column had suffered disaster. St. Petersburg telegrams indicated that the central or Samarkand forces penetrated farther than either of the other two columns; and there is strong reason for believing that the main body of the army reached Karshi, and that the advanced guard even touched the Balkh fords of the Oxus. The intelligence of this rapid advance was followed by announcements in the St. Petersburg papers that the Eastern Turkestan army had been recalled, and directly afterwards we had news of the reception of a Russian mission at Cabul. We have no more trustworthy ground for believing that the Russian forces have been recalled in their march upon the Oxus than paragraphs in the St. Petersburg papers.

The news of the arrival at Cabul of a Russian Envoy seems, at last, to have roused the English Cabinet to a sense of possible danger. The Russian Foreign Office was, therefore, interrogated as to the intentions of General Kaufmann; and so recently as July last, when General Stolieteff was already on Afghan territory, when a part of the Turkestan army was a few miles from the Afghan frontier, and the Krasnovodsk column was in full march on Kizil Arvat, a specific pledge was given that Russia had no intention to send an Envoy to Cabul, or to direct an army against the Turkomans.

The story of Russian advance is not yet complete. Her last annexation, as we have stated, was that of Khokand in 1876, but her most recent maps show a yet further advance; for she has absorbed a large part of Karateghin, and brought her frontier across the Pamir steppe to within 150 miles of Cashmere. This extension of territory is at present, probably, only on paper, but its importance, if effectually made, is indicated best by stating that it is a direct advance towards the valley of Chitral, from which the Baroghil and other passes lead into Cashmere.

CHAPTER X.

THE AFGHAN POLICY OF THE LAST TWO VICEROYS.

Resumé of Lord Northbrook's Negotiations with the Amir—Proposal to Permit Sir D. Forsyth to Return through Afghan Territory Negatived—The "Grievances" of Shere Ali—Sir Lewis Pelly's Conference with the Afghan Agent in 1876—The Occupation of Quettah—Lord Lytton's Letters to Shere Ali—The English Envoy at Ali Musjid—Repulse of the Mission—False Account Sent to England—Question of Peace or War Reverts to Consideration of Necessity of "Rectification" of Frontier—Is Refusal to Receive English Officers an Insult?—Rawlinson's Opinion of England's Policy in the Presence of Russian Agents at Cabul—Policy of English Cabinet in Sending an *Ultimatum* to Shere Ali—Lord Northbrook on the Conduct of Russia and the Amir—And on Sir James Stephen's View of the Amir's "International" Rights.

WE have now considered at some length the advances made by Russia since the Indian Mutiny in the countries round the Oxus. It remains to bring up the account of our relations with Shere Ali Khan, Amir of Afghanistan, to the present time. We have shown how, in 1873, when the agent of Shere Ali visited Lord Northbrook at Simla, he made what seemed then to be extravagant demands, and declined to enter into reciprocal engagements.

We pointed out, too, that, shortly after the Simla Conference, when he found England wanted a *quid pro quo* in return for the subsidies and protection she was willing to give, that *quid pro quo* taking the form chiefly of the reception of an English Envoy at Cabul, Shere Ali entered into a correspondence with General Kaufmann, the Russian Governor-General of Tashkend.

Lord Northbrook, in his exposition of his own and his predecessor's policy, at a public dinner at Winchester, on November 12th, 1878, gave the following explanation of the refusal of Shere Ali to receive English officers, and, as the point is important, we quote his statement at length. After disclaiming any idea of discussing matters that the Government might wish to keep secret, he continued as follows :— " On one matter I may say a word without any indiscretion, and that is about European officers ; and here I would refer to Sir Douglas Forsyth and his suggested return to India through Afghanistan. I saw the Prime Minister of Shere Ali in 1873, feeling as I did that occasions might arise when it would be of great advantage that English officers might be sent through Afghanistan, particularly as there were some questions about the frontier which we desired to have known in the interests of Afghanistan by British officers. I desired the Foreign Secretary of the Government to consult with the Prime Minister of Shere Ali to ascertain whether he would be likely to receive English officers if he was asked to do so, and a confidential communication took place accordingly. Shere Ali's Prime Minister of that time is now dead; therefore I can see no impropriety in making known his opinion. This is the opinion of the Amir of Cabul's Prime Minister in 1873, in reference to the stationing of British officers in Cabul. Speaking as a friend, and in the interest of the British Government, he could not recommend a specific request being made to station British officers in certain places. Such a demand, however friendly the Amir might be, would give rise to distrust and misapprehension. The reasons he gave were that the Afghans were deplorably ignorant, and entertained an idea that a deputation of British agents is always a precursor to annexation. He also said there was a strong party in Cabul opposed to the Amir entering into intimate relations with the British Government. Soon after that the question whether Sir Douglas Forsyth should return to India through Afghanistan, or not, came up, and the Amir regretted that he could not be allowed to return; giving as a reason that shortly before a British officer, Colonel M'Donald, had been shot on the frontier by the Afghans—a circumstance which had occasioned considerable inconvenience to the country, and inclined him to say that he could not be answerable for the safety of any English officers. I felt I had no right under the circumstances, and under the assurances which had been given by Lord Mayo that British officers should not be sent against the opinion of the Amir, to consider that any offence had been committed against the British Government."

There is no doubt, however, that Shere Ali sulked, and refused, indeed, for a time to take the very handsome subsidy of £120,000 and 15,000 rifles which were offered him.

The Amir's "grievances," which began with our recognising his brother's before his own accession, and were increased by our refusing in 1869 to guarantee the succession to his dominion of Abdulla Jan, his favourite son, received an addition in 1871 in the result of an arbitration which the Indian Government had undertaken between Persia and Afghanistan concerning the boundary of Seistan. The result was a compromise, which, as often happens, was satisfactory to neither party, and Shere Ali resented it deeply as an infringement of his sovereignty, which, as he erroneously held, the Indian Government was bound to preserve unimpaired. Again, in 1875, in return for courtesies shown by the Ruler of Wakham, a vassal of Shere Ali, towards the British Mission to Yarkand, a letter and gifts were sent by the Viceroy without previous reference to the Amir. This Shere Ali resented as another breach of his sovereignty. But the supposed slight was manifestly nothing worse than an oversight, and if our diplomatic relations with Cabul had been in a more satisfactory condition, it would never have occurred.

Sir Lewis Pelly's conference with Shere Ali's agent at Peshawar in 1876 is the only other communication the Indian Government has had with the Amir until the recent one with reference to Sir Neville Chamberlain's intended mission. What passed at the Peshawar Conference is not known, the British Government not having thought fit to make it known yet to Parliament or the public. Mr. Gladstone, Lord Lawrence, and others, have complained of the delay in doing so, as it prevents the possibility of a sound opinion being formed on the merits or demerits, the wisdom or unwisdom, of the recent policy of the Indian Government.*

But it is understood that Sir Lewis Pelly was authorised by the Viceroy (Lord Northbrook) to offer to the Amir's envoy the treaty and guarantee which Shere Ali had previously sought in 1869 and 1873, on the condition that British officers should have access to points of the Amir's frontier exposed to Russia. It was not, however, proposed to establish a British agent at Cabul, for it was already known that such a proposal would prove unacceptable to the Amir. The conference proved abortive. Shere

* See Publishers' Note prefixed.

Ali's envoy recapitulated the grievances of which his sovereign complained, but suggested no way of removing them, or of establishing better relations; at the same time, though he professed to have no authority to conclude a definite treaty, he declared that Shere Ali held the British Government pledged under any circumstances to protect his territory. We must assume, however, that he was left in no doubt, when the conference came to an end, as to the view which the Indian Government took of its own obligations towards Afghanistan.

The occupation of Quettah has been the last of the Amir's "grievances" which we have caused to exist. It had for years been contemplated as necessary to the security of our position in India that we should command the entrance to the Bolan Pass. Quettah is not in Afghan territory, but is in Baluchistan, and we occupied it in 1876 with the full consent of the Khan of Kelat, to whom it belongs. The Amir does not seem to have objected to our policy of making Quettah an advanced military post before it was accomplished, but now he is said to have made it a ground of complaint.

All we need say here of Lord Lytton's most recent action is that he sent letters to the Amir almost directly after the news reached him of the reception of a Russian mission demanding that an English mission should be also received. The death of Abdulla Jan, the heir-apparent, having occurred before an answer was received, Lord Lytton despatched a second letter, stating that the English mission would be delayed till the days of mourning were over. On the 21st September, no answer having been received from Cabul, General Sir Neville Chamberlain advanced, according to orders from Simla, into the Khaibar Pass.

The following account of what passed on that occasion is taken from the *Pioneer*, a newspaper which is sometimes spoken of (with what truth we cannot say) as the organ of the Indian Goverment:

" On the afternoon of Friday, the 20th, everything having been ready for a move for some days, it was announced that orders to march to Jamrud would probably be issued about midnight. Accordingly at 1 a.m. the word came; tents were struck, camels and mules loaded, and long before daybreak the escort, with the whole impedimenta of the Mission, saving only the personal baggage of Sir Neville Chamberlain and his staff, were on the move. Many of your readers may know the road from Peshawar to Jamrud, beyond which it has been given to few to pass. For the first three or four miles it lies due west, through rich cultivation and groves of young *sissoo* trees, to Burj-i-Hari Singh, a tower where a picket under ordinary circumstances warns peaceful travellers that if they venture further west it is at the risk of their lives. Beyond Burj-i-Hari Singh a bare, gravelly desert stretches to the foot of the Khaiber Hills, some seven or eight miles off. Three miles from the mouth of the Pass lies the half-ruined fort of Jamrud, a somewhat picturesque structure, lying just inside British territory, and held for us by the chief of a village in the neighbouring plain. Just to the east of its crumbling towers our not very pretentious camp was pitched. The total number of souls with the Mission amounted to something under a thousand, of whom eleven were British officers, four native gentlemen, and 234 fighting men, natives of the escort. The rest were camp-followers, including over 200 people, camel-drivers and others, belonging to the Commissariat, which carried nine days' rations for man and beast. The carriage consisted of 315 camels, about 250 mules, and 40 horses. The whole would have formed a *cortège* considerably over a mile in length. Conflicting reports had been brought to Peshawar as to the intentions of the Amir's officials to admit or refuse passage to the Mission; and opinions differed as to the probability of our passing Ali Musjid. The one thing certain was the presence at that place for the last two days of the Mir Akhor, the sourest old fanatic in Afghanistan, and the bitterest enemy of the Kafir, English, or Russ. It was difficult to imagine any reason for his presence, except doubt on the Amir's part as to the firmness of the commandant of Ali Musjid, Faiz Muhammad Khan, Ghilzai, in excluding the Mission. Under these circumstances Sir Neville Chamberlain considered that it would be unwise to send the whole convoy into the Pass, where even the stoppage in front, necessary during the *pour parler* certain to take place under any circumstances, must necessarily cause great confusion ; and where anything like an immediate resource to their weapons to prevent the passage of the Mission on the part of the garrison of Ali Musjid would probably lead to a panic and possibly a disaster. His Excellency, therefore, ordered Major Cavagnari to ride on towards Ali Musjid as soon as possible after the arrival of the camp at Jamrud, taking with him only a small escort of the Guides, and the headmen of our own frontier villages, and of the friendly Khaibaris. Thus attended he was to proceed until met by armed resistance, or by positive assurances on the part of the Amir's officials that they would prevent the passage of the Mission by force. A message was sent on some hours ahead to inform Faiz Muhammad Khan of Major Cavagnari's approach. It should be premised that the Khaibaris on our side of the Pass, that is, between Ali Musjid and the mouth, had promised that no opposition on their part, or on that of their friends, should deter the Mission, or its advanced guard, from being brought face to face with the Amir's officials.

This, of course, was a matter of the very highest importance, as preventing the possibility of excuses of non-responsibility.

"Somewhere about nine in the morning Major Cavagnari left Jamrud; with him were Colonel Jenkins of the Guides, commanding the escort, Captain Wigram Battye, and twenty-four sowars. Three miles from camp the little party entered the Pass, and shortly afterwards met the messenger to Faiz Muhammad returning with an answer, begging them not to advance, &c. Of this, of course, no notice was taken, and a ride of four or five miles over the capital road made by Mackeson in 1840 and still passable for heavy artillery, brought them in sight of Ali Musjid, a picturesque little fort, perched on a precipitous hill overhanging the valley through which flowed a little stream. From the lofty hills to the right, two parallel spurs of half the height of the fort abutted on the road; and on the nearest of these Major Cavagnari and his party took their stand, sending forward a messenger to announce their arrival. Directly they were perceived, the walls of the fort were manned; and shortly afterwards, seeing that no advance was made, a number of the garrison left its protection and lined the opposite ridge. It was then evident that the reports that had reached Peshawar about the substitution of regular troops for the irregular levies usually forming the garrison were false, and that the warriors in front were only matchlockmen. The distance to the fort, a mile or more down one hill and up another, made the exchange of messages tedious; a couple of hours passed without any appearance of a satisfactory result; and Major Cavagnari was beginning to abandon any hope of meeting a responsible official of the Amir face to face, and had begun to prepare an ultimatum, when a messenger arrived bearing the welcome news that Faiz Muhammad Khan would come out to meet Major Cavagnari and three others at an indicated spot by the side of the stream halfway between the two ridges. Shortly afterwards he was seen approaching, and Major Cavagnari, taking with him Colonel Jenkins and two of his men, went down the hill to meet Faiz Muhammad, accompanied by the headman of the tribes and of the British frontier villages, Captain Battye and the rest of the Guides remaining on the ridge. On his way the chief of one of the other Khaibar tribes, friendly to, or at least in the pay of, the Amir, made a show of stopping him, saying that he had more than the stipulated three men with him; but Major Cavagnari put him aside, saying that he had not come to talk with him, but with the Amir's people; and nothing further was said. On nearing each other the two parties dismounted, Major Cavagnari and Faiz Muhammad shook hands, and the former remarked that the place appointed for the interview was inconvenient, and suggested a grove of trees near a watermill close by. This was accepted, and the two parties sat down, surrounded by a couple of hundred or so of Faiz Muhammad's ruffianly band. The conversation, after the usual friendly greetings, was opened by Major Cavagnari, who said that Faiz Muhammad and he were equally servants of their respective Governments, and therefore only carrying out their orders. There was thus no necessity for the discussion being carried on in any but a friendly spirit; that he, Faiz Muhammad must be aware of the presence and intended advance of the Mission; and that Sir Neville Chamberlain had sent the speaker on to ascertain from his own lips whether he had orders to admit or stop the Mission. If there were any latitude in his orders, he felt sure that Faiz Muhammad would be aware of the heavy responsibility he would incur by preventing the advance of the Mission, as his act in so doing would be taken as that of the Amir himself. Faiz Muhammad replied that he himself was also actuated by friendly feelings towards Major Cavagnari, whom he had great pleasure in meeting for the first time, in proof of which he pointed out that he might, instead of coming down to meet Major Cavagnari, have ordered his men to fire on the party when it appeared. He then went on to say that he had been severely reprimanded for letting Nawab Gholan Husain (the Viceroy's native envoy) pass, and how, therefore, could he risk the responsibility of permitting the advance of the Mission? He then begged that Sir Neville Chamberlain would halt a few days till he could communicate with Cabul. This, Major Cavagnari replied, was not only impossible but unnecessary, as the Cabul authorities had long been aware of the approach of the Mission. The conversation continued in this strain for some little time, Major Cavagnari urging the weight of the responsibility Faiz Muhammad would incur, and the latter repeating his inability to allow the Mission to pass without direct orders from Cabul. At last, on the Englishman again pointing out the friendly character of the Mission, the Afghan, showing for the first time some warmth, said:—'Is this friendliness, to stir up dissension in the Amir's dominions by bribing his subjects to disobey his orders by bringing you and others here?' alluding to the negotiations carried on with the Khaibaris for the safe-conduct first of the Nawab and afterwards of the Mission. At this an ambiguous murmur was heard from the crowd, and Major Cavagnari turned the subject by saying that was not a matter for subordinates to discuss, and that if His Highness the Amir had any complaint to make, no doubt the British Government would give him a satisfactory reply. He then asked Faiz Muhammad for a final answer; whether he was distinctly to understand that the Mission would be resisted by force should it advance the next morning. To this Faiz Muhammad replied that he had no alternative but to use force, if necessary. On this Major Cavagnari asked the chiefs with him, if they considered this a sufficiently clear answer, to which they replied that it was so. He then, thanking Faiz Muhammad for the courteous and friendly spirit that he had shown, hoped that they might meet under more agreeable circumstances, shook hands with him, and departed. It should be noticed that, though the Mir Akhor did not show himself, his deputy was present at the meeting, but without speaking.

"Major Cavagnari and his party at once came back to the camp at Jumrud, whence he rode on to Peshawar to communicate the result of his Mission to the Envoy, who returned with him to Jamrud late in the evening. At day-break the next morning orders were issued for an immediate return to Peshawar. Before leaving Sir Neville Chamberlain assembled the friendly Khaibaris, and told them that the stipulated reward would be paid them exactly as if the Mission had passed through the Khaibar; and that he promised them in the name of the British Government, whose word they knew they could trust, that as long as there remained a rupee in the treasury, or a sepoy in the army, they should be protected from any retaliation by the Amir or his officers."

Thus ended the Cabul Mission.

It is not too much to say that England was convulsed by a different version of the interview which appeared in the letter of the Indian correspondent of the *Times* on the 23rd of September, which made it appear that the English officers had been insulted and threatened. Later on, the true account came to us, and calmer feeling prevailed. The question then reverted to the older phase of the policy, which took the form of pushing forward (or "rectifying") our frontier, instead of the more urgent one of having an insult to avenge; unless, as some think, the reception of a Russian Mission renders the refusal to receive an English one an insult. On this latter point it is of interest to notice that Sir Henry Rawlinson, as long ago as 1874, contemplated the possibility of Russia sending an envoy to Cabul, and discussed the probable policy England would pursue. He said (note on page 366 of "England and Russia in the East"), speaking of Prince Gortchakoff's official intimation to Lord Granville, that it was undesirable that Russian agents should go to Cabul, "It is quite possible, however, in the sequel, if matters should become at all complicated, that this subject may be revived, and Russia may wish to have a Mission at Cabul. *Diplomatically, perhaps, we could hardly* *object to such an arrangement, but we might, at any rate, insist on sending at the same time an English Mission to Bokhara.*" The italics are ours. We do not know yet what communications have passed between the Russian Government and our own; nor is it certain that the conflict, if there is to be one, will be confined to a duel between British India and the barbarous State on her frontier, or will be extended to embrace England and Russia, and thus do what has been so often threatened—light up two continents with the torch of war.* The action of the English Cabinet in giving the Amir another opportunity of retreating from the perilous position in which his recent conduct has placed him has been much criticised.

But the majority of people will, in the end, we think, at least, commend the policy of sending a final message—an *ultimatum*, as it is termed—before proceeding to hostilities, whatever may be the opinion held as to the original policy which has led up to the present situation. On the 26th of October that message was sent by Lord Lytton—not to Cabul itself, as that would, it was thought, compromise the safety of a British subject—but to the fort of Ali Musjid, in the Khaibar Pass, and was there delivered to the Amir's officer. Its purport is generally believed to have been in effect a repetition

* See Publishers' Note prefixed.

of the terms offered by Sir Lewis Pelly, with the intimation that an answer must be returned before the 20th November, in order to avert a declaration of war.

The following opinion on the conduct of Russia and of Afghanistan, given by Lord Northbrook in the speech before referred to, seems to deserve attention. He said:—"It would appear at first sight that by sending a Mission to Cabul they had distinctly broken through the engagements they had made; but we must be fair in this matter, and we must recollect that it is not so long ago—towards the spring of the year—that unfortunately we were on the brink of a war with Russia. It was supposed that Russia would not submit to the terms of the San Stefano Treaty. We all know that the British Government took a decided line against Russia. Assuming such an attitude, we sent troops to Malta; and in point of fact it was generally supposed that the question of peace and war hung at that time on a thread. For my own part, I do not hesitate to say that if we had the right, as I hold that we had the right, to send native troops to Malta, the Russians had the right to take such steps as they thought necessary to protect Russian territory in Asia. This is the explanation which I give, and which I conceive to be the natural explanation of the movement of troops in the spring of this year, and the sending of the Mission to Afghanistan. I have seen it mentioned in the newspapers that this Mission to Cabul was sent after the signature of the Treaty of Berlin, and that this shows the animosity of the Russian Government towards us. That statement can at any rate be disputed. The Russian Mission arrived at Cabul on the 22nd July. The road from Samarkand consists of marches extending over a distance of 620 miles. It could not have been possible for the Russian Mission to march from Samarkand in less than a month. It was therefore impossible that a Mission starting on the 13th of July could arrive on the 22nd of July. That issue was disposed of by the mere question of distance. Now, it seems to me, with regard to the question of Russia in this matter, to be quite clear that the Government of this country had a right, peace being declared, to enter into a diplomatic correspondence with Russia for the purpose of asking what were her intentions, and saying that we should like to know now whether she would adhere to the formal arrangements with respect to interference with Afghanistan, or what her policy was to be. That the Government had a perfect right to do, and my own impression is that that is the course which the Government really has pursued. We do not know all that. What we do know is that papers were promised the day before

Parliament separated, and I have no doubt that those papers will soon be produced. So far, then, as to the conduct of Russia. Now as regards the Amir of Afghanistan. Supposing that Shere Ali had, when I was Governor-General of India, received a Russian Mission at Cabul without first consulting the British Government as to whether it should be received, I should say that that was an unfair act, in consequence of our previous arrangement with him; but now we must look at the circumstances which went before the case. As it has actually arisen, it was impossible for the Amir to communicate with the British Government, for, rightly or wrongly, our agent at his Court had been withdrawn. We know, however, that he tried to prevent the Russian Mission going to Cabul. That has appeared several times in the papers, and through other impartial sources, and I believe it to be the fact. We cannot possibly have any evidence that the Amir has entered into any hostile arrangement with the Russian Embassy after having received them. I have no fear of Russian intrigue in Afghanistan. From all that I know or have ever heard of that country, the real feeling of the Amir of Cabul and Afghanistan is a feeling of independence, a dislike of any interference, either by England or by Russia, in his affairs; and I will say this much, that when I left India, the Amir, though he would have disliked any interference on the part of England, would have resented any shown by Russia to a far greater extent. Therefore, if Russia's people be in the country they will only arouse more feelings of independence, and the longer they remain the more influence will they lose. But when we are considering the conduct of Shere Ali in this matter, I confess that I have observed with the greatest regret opinions which have been expressed by the Press with regard to it; and what I regret more is, that Sir James Stephen, a Liberal leader, has laid down a principle with which I can in no way agree. Sir James Stephen has contended that the principles of international law have no reference to our dealings with Shere Ali. He says that there is no law by which the case between Shere Ali and ourselves can be tried. We are exceedingly powerful and highly civilised. He is comparatively weak and half-barbarous. He cannot be permitted to follow a course of policy which may expose us to danger, and we are to be the judges of the cause, and we are to decide according to our own interests. I have given you Sir James Stephen's own words, as I do not wish to misrepresent him. For where does the doctrine he lays down go? Why it goes this length, that any nation —any civilised nation it must be—in dealing with another weak nation, and one they conceive to be uncivilised, may act on no other principle than their might. This principle would justify the partition of Poland, and would justify every act of Russia against which this country has been crying out for some time. I feel sure that Sir James Stephen cannot know the meaning of what he has said, and that such a doctrine as this must shock the moral sense of all rightly-feeling people of this country. Sir James Stephen has confounded the conventional law of nations, and the law of nations which depends on the practice of the Western States, with those fundamental principles of the law of nations that are founded on the first principles of morals, and are derived from what Bacon calls the Fountains of Justice, and which have been recognised not only by Christian lawyers and statesmen, but by heathen lawyers and statesmen, from long time past."

Lord Northbrook further pointed out that such a lax view of international law is especially dangerous in India, where we have treaty engagements with many semi-civilised States. He protested strongly against such doctrines, and expressed an opinion that, if propounded in Parliament, they would be instantly repudiated.

APPENDIX A.

NEW ROUTE TO INDIA.

THE following note on the proposed new route to India may be of interest at this time :—

"Consul-General Nixon, sending to the Foreign Office the Bagdad trade returns for the Turkish official year ending in March, 1878, observes that the country is capable of unlimited development, and one of the first steps to this end would be the construction of a railway between Bagdad and the foot of the Persian hills, and another from Bagdad to Alexandretta *via* Mosul. This would give an alternative route to India, and be more expeditious than *via* the Suez Canal. Swift steamers from Kurrachee would reach Busreh (1,547 miles) in six days; from Busreh to Bagdad river steamers would run with ease in 72 hours, and at the outside another 60 hours by rail would land passengers on the shores of the Mediterranean; and this period of $11\frac{1}{2}$ days is capable of acceleration. A railway from Busreh to Bagdad might be an after consideration, as the river Tigris affords a highway which, if traversed by steamers of higher power than those now used, would much reduce the time occupied in the transit. The Consul considers that a railway from Bagdad to Alexandretta would pay exceedingly well, and British commerce would benefit greatly, as Bagdad would become the great mart, and drive Russian goods out of the Persian and Southern Asian markets, owing to the expensive land carriage those goods would have to defray. The cost of a railway from Busreh, at the head of the Persian Gulf, to Alexandretta on the Mediterranean has been estimated at £7,225,000, but this is at the rate of £8,500 per mile, a high rate considering that there is water carriage from London to Bagdad for railway material. Deducting the distance from Busreh to Bagdad, which is 250 miles as the crow flies, the first expenditure would be reduced to £5,100,000 on the 600 miles from Bagdad to Alexandretta. The country between Bagdad and Mosul is a dead level. The expenditure on bridges would be inconsiderable. Bridging the Tigris, indeed, might be avoided, if the terminus were made on the right bank of the river at Bagdad, and from thence ran straight to Aleppo, the line being flanked on one side by the Tigris and on the other by the Euphrates, and nearly the whole route a flat. The Consul suggests that the civilising influences which a railway through Arabia would initiate are considerable, and that the development of the country, with its vast resources and its enormous ancient system of canal irrigation, is well worthy the attention of statesmen. The privilege of navigating the Tigris from Busreh to Bagdad would have to be acquired from the Turkish Government; at present they have a few steamers of their own on the river, and are jealous of other nations entering into competition."

APPENDIX B.

RUSSIA AND ENGLAND IN ASIA.

THE following estimate of the relative positions of Russia and England in the East is from the pen of Major-General Sir John Adye, in a reply to a letter by Sir James Stephen, and a better exposition of the subject in a few words could hardly be given :—

"First, as to the general position of Russia in Central Asia. Sir James Stephen in his remarks compares it with that which we held in India in 1803 under Lord Wellesley, and, although he does not ignore the isolated and precarious position of the Russian troops in the Central Asian deserts, he still appears to think that by raising armies and by forming alliances they may gradually develop into a great Power there, and thus become a danger to us in India. But the circumstances are almost entirely different. India and Central Asia do not compare with each other. The former is a fertile country, and rich in military resources—that is, in warlike races, in food, forage, fuel, and, nowadays, in its roads and communications. It contains about 200,000,000 people, of different races and religions, of which the Muhammadans are a minority. By conquering India we have, in short, obtained a magnificent empire; one which under our rule is daily rising in prosperity. Civil government is firmly established, and the military position is far stronger than ever. Our troops, both English and Native, are well armed and trained; the arsenals are fixed at strategical points; while our internal communications by river, road, and rail are comparatively easy, and our resources are capable of almost indefinite expansion.

"Russia in Central Asia holds in virtual subjection the three great Principalities of Khiva, Bokhara, and Khokand. This is not very difficult, as their forces are mere armed rabble, and if the power of Russia in that part of the world were measured by mere geographical extent, it would be formidable; but, in truth, this very extent is the cause of great weakness. There is a general deficiency throughout the whole vast region of food, water, fuel, forage, and roads. The few rivers are difficult of navigation, and the transport is almost entirely carried on by means of camels. This latter point at once indicates the desert nature of the country, and greatly aggravates the difficulty of massing troops and stores at their outposts. The whole population of Central Asia in Russian possession does not, it is said, exceed four millions and a-half, consisting chiefly of predatory tribes thinly scattered over a vast area. They are fanatical Muhammadans, and bitterly hostile, and I have never heard that Russia has ventured to raise a single battalion on the spot. Civil government is in its infancy, and financially the country is a perpetual drain. The nearest railway-station is at Orenburg, about 1,000 miles from Samarkand, and the country between the Caspian and Tashkend is for the most part a hopeless desert. It is possible that Russia may in time, to some extent, consolidate her conquests, but the geographical features and permanent condition of the country are against her.

"I can see no analogy between the precarious position of General Kaufmann, amid barren steppes, and that of Lord Wellesley in 1803, standing in the fertile plains of Bengal. A consideration of all the circumstances would appear to prove that the present position of Russia in Central Asia is not one calculated to afford her a favourable base of operations against our dominion in India. It is very important to have a clear conception on these vital points of the comparative power of Russia and England in the East.

"For many years past that policy has been consistent, and may be described as one of conciliation, of mediation, and of subsidies. Acknowledging the strategical importance of Afghanistan, our object has been to gain the confidence and friendship of the Afghan and Belooch rulers, and also of the independent frontier tribes, in the hope that should external danger ever arise they would be on our side, and be ready to become the joint defenders with us of their mountain ranges. I always contemplate the possibility of our having to enter the country for our own defence, and it should be prepared for by conciliating and not by attacking our neighbours.

"'Masterly inactivity' is the expression commonly

used to denote the policy which for many years has prevailed. It is a misleading term, as it conveys the idea that we have washed our hands of our neighbours' concerns, whereas the real circumstances are very different. It is true we have refrained from interference in their internal feuds and battles. Unless invited to mediate, we have left them to settle their own affairs, being only anxious to see strong and quiet Governments established on our borders. With half-savage, fanatical people like the Afghans and Belooches, great difficulties have naturally arisen, but on the whole we have been successful. For instance, so long ago as January, 1857, Sir John, now Lord, Lawrence, made a treaty with Dost Muhammad, Shere Ali's father, and by a large subsidy and present of muskets induced him to drive the Persians from Herat; but another result indirectly followed from this successful effort at conciliation. The great Mutiny broke out in May, 1857; but although we were in dire extremity, and although the Punjab was considerably denuded of troops for the siege of Delhi, Dost Muhammad, though much pressed by his people, refused to allow a single Afghan to attack us in our hour of danger. That, to my judgment, is a very pregnant instance that conciliation and kindness are as likely to be successful with Afghans as with other people. Again, in 1869, the late Lord Mayo received Shere Ali with honour at Umballa, and by gifts of money and arms gave practical proofs of our friendship; and although Shere Ali may not be as reliable or as great a man as his father, there is no reason to believe that Lord Mayo's policy was other than prudent and successful. Again, in 1873, after a long diplomatic correspondence, Lord Granville induced the Russians to accept our view of the northern boundaries of Afghanistan, by which Badakshan and Wakhan were secured to Shere Ali. This was a further proof of our friendly intervention, and throughout the correspondence Prince Gortchakoff fully acknowledged that Shere Ali was legitimately under our influence, and beyond that of Russia. In all our dealings with the Belooch and Afghan frontier tribes, the same general policy has been followed for years past, and with considerable success. The border throughout its length is far quieter now than in years gone by. Occasional acts of outrage and robbery are treated as matters of police. Many of the men of the Afghan tribes beyond the border now enter our service, and do their duty well. Some hold positions of trust, and settle inside our territory. Therefore I maintain that a conciliatory policy has been in a great measure successful, and was leading straight to the object we had in view, although time, patience, and forbearance are required before the results become palpable and confirmed. I do not propose to discuss the exceptional causes which have led to our recent rupture with Shere Ali. As regards the military operations which now appear imminent, the main difficulties lie in the necessity for collecting the supplies of food, munitions, and transport at our frontier posts before we can enter the country.

Whether we advance by the Khaibar or the Bolan, our lines of communication will lie through rocky defiles, and over stony, desert tracts, deficient in food, forage, fuel, and often in water. Sir John Keane, in 1838, is said to have lost 20,000 camels between the Indus and Candahar, although his march was virtually unopposed. Looking at the fleeting nature of Afghan internal politics, to the perpetual discords which arise between the ruler at Cabul and his insubordinate chiefs, I think it very possible that Shere Ali may find he is not backed by his people, and that he may still make such concessions as will save him from the inevitable ruin which his present conduct will otherwise bring upon him. Should we, however, be compelled to advance in force, and enter on a campaign, its cost will be excessive, and the worst feature is that our chief difficulties will arise when we find ourselves in possession of the country with the feelings of the people roused against us."

APPENDIX C.

RUSSIA'S ADVANCE COMPARED WITH THAT OF ALEXANDER THE GREAT.

THE following is an extract from a letter by General M. McMurdo in the *Times* of November 5th :—

"Although 2,000 years have passed since the Macedonian Greeks broke through the passes of Afghanistan and overthrew Porus on the Jelum, the operations of war are not less practicable under the conditions of the nineteenth century than they were in the days of the Phalanx. I do not mean for one moment to assert that Russia would meet with the same ultimate success as the Greeks; what I desire to show is, that up to a certain point she has already gained the same strategical advantages as her predecessor. The progress of the Greeks through Asia was, as that of a regular army, perfect in its administration and drill, and taking along with them the highest civilisation and culture, long afterwards maintained by their colonies. I have no books here, but I am satisfied that Arrian gives ample evidence of the principles on which their advance was conducted. Thus (as an example of administration) at Babylon, where the army rested on the conclusion of the operations that succeeded the victory of Arbela,

Alexander sent home (by Aleppo, I think) the men whose term of service had expired, and the officers who conducted them brought back, in due course, the recruits to replace them. Babylon became, in short, a secondary base for his further advance; and thus, by a system of successive depôts, some of which became colonies, he effected his ultimate object of reaching India. The last of these depôt-colonies was in India itself. The site of ancient Taxila was determined some years ago to be about 14 miles north-west of Rawul Pindee; and there is still a small race or clan (now dying out) in the neighbouring hills that claims descent from these Greeks, and whose pride on this account revolts at service of any kind.

"Now, the Russian advance through Asia has been conducted hitherto upon similar principles, the chief (and perhaps only) difference being in the time occupied. There are several sufficient reasons for the more deliberate action of Russia, with which I will not occupy your space; but as Earl Grey challenges her capability of advancing because of the difficulties of transport and supplies, I may state briefly that these doubtless formed one of the chief reasons. The difference in the *impedimenta* of a modern army in Asia compared with the Greeks under Xenophon or Alexander consists in the trains of artillery and ammunition. Russia had, therefore, good reason to wait till modern science in the form of a railway would compensate for that difference. I believe I have said sufficient to show that with

Orenburg and the Caspian as a secondary base, and amply furnished magazines at Tashkend and Samarkand (and, it seems probable, Merv also), the strategical situation of the Russians in Asia is now as good as was that of the Greeks previous to their attack on the passes of Afghanistan. But if Greek had met Greek in the Khaibar, history might possibly have told a different tale. With this observation, therefore, the parallel necessarily terminates."

APPENDIX D.

LORD LAWRENCE ON THE PRESENT CRISIS.

THE following letter of Lord Lawrence appeared in the *Daily News* of October 28th, and gives very succinctly his view of the justness, or otherwise, of an invasion of Afghanistan :—

"AFGHANISTAN.

"TO THE EDITOR OF THE DAILY NEWS.

" SIR,—In the letter signed ' Pace Tua,' which appeared in the *Times* of the 26th inst., will be found this passage :—' I venture to draw attention to circumstances which point to the probability that the Amir's hostility is by no means of such recent date as that ascribed to it by Lord Lawrence, but can be traced at least as far back as the date of the Umballah Conference, when the Amir sought in vain for an assurance from the Indian Government that it would guarantee the independence of Afghanistan, and for the acknowledgment of the son as his successor whom he had selected as his heir ; while the payment of the annual donation of money and arms which Lord Lawrence had unfortunately commenced was at the same time discontinued.' That a change of policy such as is here indicated was then made has more than once been asserted on the one hand, and denied on the other. I will endeavour to show that in point of fact no such change then took place, and that the ₁real change in the conduct of the Government of India towards the Amir, in all essential points, dates back so far as April, 1876, when Lord Northbrook resigned the Government into the hands of the present Viceroy. I would not at this time press the consideration of the change of policy on the public, except that on a due appreciation of it depends whether the people of England are in a position to form a just estimate of the conduct of Shere Ali in refusing to receive Sir Neville Chamberlain's mission. If we wait until it pleases the Ministry to give the public all the information which they can supply on all points connected with the rebuff we have received, we may wait, as I have formerly said, until it can be of no practical value to obtain it.

"I desire to prevent war between England and Afghanistan, and I can have no hope of doing so unless I can show to the minds of impartial men that such a war would be unjust; and this I have no hope of doing unless these papers are produced. In the meantime, I am restricted to arguing on the probabilities of the case. To refer, then, to the statements of 'Pace Tua,' above quoted. I reply that though the Amir may have been disappointed in regard to a refusal to comply with these proposals, he could not have anticipated success, for he must have been well aware that so far back as 1854—55, when our treaty with the Afghan Government was signed by his full brother, Sirdar Hydur Khan, and myself, the Government of India had refused to make an offensive and defensive treaty with Afghanistan.

"In the second place, Amir Shere Ali may possibly have believed that we should give him a formal guarantee recognising his favourite son as his successor. I know not what actually took place at the Durbar at Umballah in 1869; but, assuming that Lord Mayo did refuse to guarantee the succession, he did so no doubt by authority received from England; and that there was reason in such a refusal ought to be obvious to every man conversant with Oriental customs and habits of thought. Even to recognise, let alone to guarantee, the succession of a particular son is, in the eyes of an Asiatic ruler, to bind a Government to maintain that which they have recognised. Thus we should in this case have been compelled, if necessary, to sustain the authority of the Amir's son by force of arms; and we would not have done this without being prepared to act against the wishes of the majority of the people of Afghanistan—a line of policy which the Amir knew well we had sound reasons for not pursuing, and which his own father had deprecated in earnest terms to me in 1857. There still remains the question whether Lord Mayo's refusal of his request caused serious offence to the Amir. I do not think so; first, because I believe—I write under correction—that he never expressed an opinion of this kind, and assuredly he is a chief who is not particularly reticent by nature ; and, secondly, because at the time he left Umballah to return to Cabul, the newspapers in India were full of statements of the satisfaction which the Amir had felt and expressed at his reception.

"Then comes the point whether my gift of arms and money to Shere Ali in 1867 was unfortunate, that is to say, impolitic. I believe that it was not so. The arrangement was approved of by the Secretary of State for India at the time. People who from their knowledge of the Afghan question had even thought that the Government of India was wrong in not supporting Shere Ali in the contest between himself and his brothers for the throne of Cabul, and who may generally be considered the advocates for an active and interfering policy, cannot really object to our having thus assisted him. And these gifts were not volunteered, but granted on his especial application; showing that the struggle through which he had passed had bereft him of resources, and had left him no choice but to apply to us for help. Again, as a matter of fact, I did not grant the Amir an annual subsidy—it was a single gift which I made on the part of the British Government, and its renewal from time to time was to be dependent on the Government of India's satisfaction with his conduct. This arrangement was considered more likely to work well than if we had granted Shere Ali an annual subsidy—a subsidy which we could not justly intermit without showing specific reasons for so doing. It seems unreasonable to suppose that this grant of money and arms had an unfortunate influence on the Amir's mind. No money has, since the Umballah Conference, been given to him, except some two lacs of rupees by Lord Northbrook, and ten lacs which this Viceroy offered, and which the Amir refused.

"It is true that previous to the arrival of the present Viceroy the Amir appears to have taken offence on account of the decision in the Seistan boundary dispute, which he is said to have considered very adverse to his rights and interests; and it was on that account that Lord Northbrook proposed to give him a grant of money—not that it was thought that his interests had not been duly regarded in the above decision, but simply with the generous intention of softening his mind, which appeared to be brooding over the subject.

"The Amir was also said to have felt aggrieved at a request made to him, that some of the English officers returning from the Yarkand Mission might be permitted to journey to India by way of Wakhan and Cabul. Another alleged grievance was that the Viceroy had sent the Governor of Wakhan a small present in recognition of his politeness to the officers above mentioned. But these two cases were in their nature trivial and unimportant, and cannot really be supposed to have irritated the Amir, more particularly as in neither case were the wishes of the Viceroy pressed on him.

"'Pace Tua' asks what other course was to be

pursued than 'that of sending a Mission to Cabul, unless we were prepared to leave Russia in undisturbed possession of the field.' Considering the wayward and jealous disposition of Shere Ali, ready to take offence at trifles light as air, the best course was to leave him alone for a time. It did not follow, therefore, that we were indifferent, or neglectful, of what Russia might be doing in Afghanistan.

"The Amir's real grievance arose from several causes which I have stated in former letters, such as the occupation of Quettah, the pressing on him of a Mission to Cabul with the view of placing English officers in various parts of the country as a more or less permanent measure, the withdrawal of our native agent from that city, and our not sending any one of the same character to take his place, the arming of the Kashmere troops with arms of precision, and the directions given to their chiefs to watch the passes leading to Chitral, and the embargo laid on the export of arms, &c., from India to Cabul.

"It has been lately stated that the Conference at Peshawar between Sir Lewis Pelly and the Amir's Agent took place somewhere about six months before the occupation of Quettah, and that it could not therefore have been one of the causes of the failure of that Conference. But if the readers of the *Daily News* will refer to the Blue-Book 'Biluchistan,' No. 2, page 324, they will find by comparison of dates that the occupation of Quettah preceded and did not follow that Conference. From a letter of Captain Scott, commanding the detachment of the

4th Sikh Infantry, it is shown that he arrived at Quettah on the 2nd November, 1876, and began marking out barracks for his men on the 5th of that month, whereas the Conference at Peshawar began towards the end of December of that year, and is stated in the *Times* of the 21st inst. as taking place in January, 1877.

"In what I have now said I by no means intend to place the rupture of our amicable relations with the Afghans solely on the shoulders of the present Viceroy of India. What I desire to convey is that the causes which led to that rupture really arose after his assumption of the Government, and that our previous relations with the chiefs of that country were on the whole of a friendly nature.

" In what proportion the responsibility of the state of things in Afghanistan is to be divided between the Viceroy and the Ministry of the day, time and the production of the correspondence can alone show.

" Yours faithfully,

" LAWRENCE.

" *Stone House, St. Peter's,*
" *Isle of Thanet, Oct.* 28."

APPENDIX E.

SALE'S DEFENCE OF JALALABAD.

THE following account of General Sale's gallant defence of Jalalabad is taken from the *Daily News* of 30th September, 1878, and is quoted here as a very complete summary of that noble achievement:—

" Few of the many gallant feats of British soldiers can compare with General Sale's gallant and successful defence of Jalalabad. After the deeply disheartening news had reached him that the Cabul force, under General Elphinstone, had been cut to pieces in the defiles, Sale, throughout that terrible winter, bated no jot of heart or hope, and his example is the more remarkable since it establishes the truth that the calamity which had befallen our soldiers might have been avoided if wiser counsels and a more resolute policy had been adopted. During our two years' occupation of Afghanistan, nothing had been more clearly proved than the fact that the native races were unable to withstand a resolute attack either from British troops or Sepoys led by British officers. Treachery and ambush, intrigue and assassination, were still their chosen modes of offence ; and, though they had hovered about our famished and enfeebled soldiers and camp-followers, and assailed them cautiously in moments of difficulty and embarrassment with only too much effect, the very last remnant of our forces had again and again put their assailants to flight. In the face of these circumstances, it is impossible not to concur in Sir John Kaye's opinion that the true policy of General Elphinstone was not to capitulate and retreat, but to strengthen his positions in Cabul, and endeavour to obtain supplies by bold sorties and incursions into the surrounding country. Such, in fact, were the tactics of General Sale, by which, even after receipt of intelligence of the disasters of the Koord Cabul, he was enabled to maintain himself and protect his army against all the efforts of Akbar Khan to obtain possession of the fortress.

"A less cautious commander might easily have been betrayed into a step which would have been no less fatal than the evacuation of Cabul. Only a few days before that event, and while as yet there was no token of the calamity that ensued, a band of strange horsemen had suddenly presented themselves at the gates of the town. They carried a flag of truce, and described themselves as the bearers of a letter from Cabul. Conducted into the presence of General Sale, the strangers presented their missive, which proved to be a despatch written in English, and signed by General Elphinstone himself. Its contents were startling and extraordinary; but of the genuineness of the document there could be no question. It conveyed the intelligence of the convention that had been entered into with Akbar, and directed General Sale forthwith to march with arms, stores, and ammunition for Peshawar. In brief, General Sale's superior ordered an immediate retreat in the depth of winter by the ominous Khaibar Pass, accompanying his instructions with the assurance that 'our troops would not be molested on the way.' It is needless to say that the writer had no sufficient grounds for such an assurance. The evacuation of Jalalabad had simply been wrung from him as one of the conditions of the protection which was promised, but was never intended to be accorded ; and, though General Elphinstone proved his faith in the word of his foe, and suffered the penalty of his confidence, the order was not the less remarkable for the weakness and infatuation that it displayed. Peremptory as the directions were, and serious as was the responsibility of neglecting to obey, Sale nevertheless wisely took the latter course. A council of war was held, at which it was formally resolved that 'it would not be prudent to act upon such a document, and that the garrison would, therefore, remain where it was until further orders.' This timely act of disobedience unquestionably saved the army under Sale from certain destruction. At the very moment when the council was deliberating the deep snows of the Koord Cabul were crimson with the blood of the struggling mass who were vainly endeavouring to make their way through, to rejoin their more fortunate comrades at less than a hundred miles distance. There can be no question that the despatch that had been extorted from the sick and feeble commander-in-chief formed part of a cunning scheme, the aim of which was to give to the destruction of the Feringhees a degree of completeness, and an air of sudden and overwhelming retribution, which could not but affect powerfully the imagination of any future expedition to be despatched for the invasion of the Afghan territory. Instead of capitulating, Sale set to work to dig trenches round the bastions of the town, and to drill every camp follower capable of bearing arms. Only three days after this bold and energetic determination was taken, a sentry upon the walls on the side towards Gundamack called aloud that he saw 'a mounted man in the distance.' Glasses were out in a moment; and there was clearly to be seen, sitting upon a half-starved pony, a rider who appeared to be a European, and was manifestly faint or wounded. Long before the stranger reached the walls a foreboding of his melancholy story was in the hearts of the defenders. It was Dr. Brydon—not the only survivor of the final horrors of the Jagdullah, but certainly the only one who had escaped to convey the news. He was bleeding, faint, and covered with wounds, but still grasping in his right hand his only weapon of defence—a small fragment of a sword.

"Nothing could now seem more forlorn than the position of the defenders of Jalalabad, surrounded by the triumphant Afghans and entirely cut off from communication with Peshawar. That their late comrades were destroyed they well knew. On the first news of their fate, Sale ordered the cavalry to mount forthwith, and to patrol along the Cabul road to the farthest reach which might seem to be compatible with their own safety. Many officers accompanied them. In the striking words of Mr. Gleig, 'They had not ridden above four miles from the town ere they came upon the mutilated remains of the three out of Dr. Brydon's four ill-fated companions, of whom he could give no account. Not a straggler, however—not a living soul, man, woman, or child—appeared either there, or as far as the eye could reach beyond. Wherefore the patrol, after lingering about till the shadows began to deepen, turned their horses' heads with sorrow homewards, and rejoined their comrades. That night lanterns were suspended from poles at different points about the ramparts ; while from time to time the bugles sounded the advance, in the hope that one or other of these beacons might guide some wanderer to a place of rest. But none came ; and though on the morrow, and for several days and nights subsequently a like course was pursued, not one man, European or native, seemed to be alive—certainly none profited by it.' On the side of Peshawar no adequate preparations had been made in view of troubles so unexpected ; nor did any succour come. The first thought was to increase the stock of provisions. While the non-combatants trained to handle pikes manufactured out of old hooks and any other available bits of iron that could be found, were assigned to duty on the ramparts, foraging parties were sent forth, who in two days brought back with them 170 head of cattle and between 600 and 700 sheep. The cattle were slaughtered immediately, and salted down, as fodder was wanting; the sheep were sent out every morning to graze in the marshes between the river and the town walls, attended by shepherds and an armed covering-party. Every tree and bush which could afford cover for marksmen was cut down, and all the doors and timber-work from the houses outside the walls were carried off and laid up as winter fuel. About the end of the month numerous bodies of the enemy were observed marching in various directions, and on the morning of the 15th, instead of the welcome sight of the advanced guard of General Pollock's army of relief, they beheld the white tents of Akbar Khan on the farther side of the river, about six miles distant from the walls. Still the men laboured cheerfully in the ditches and on the ramparts. The works were daily becoming stronger; but their labours were destined to be frustrated by an enemy more swift and destructive than any they had yet encountered in Afghanistan. On the 19th the men marched out as usual, with their pickaxes and spades; the guards were at the gates, the sentries on the walls. Colonel Monteith, the field officer for the day, had ascended one of the bastions, and was scanning the horizon with his glass, when suddenly the ground trembled, and a noise was heard which is described as not so much like thunder as the sound of a thousand heavily-laden waggons rolling and jolting over an ill-paved street. The

Appendix E.

diggers looked around 'them with a stare of consternation; and then, as if actuated by one common influence, the parties in the trenches, seizing their arms, rushed out. It was well for them that they did so; for scarcely had they reached the glacis ere the whole of the plain began to heave like billows on the surface of the ocean, and walls and houses, splitting asunder, came tumbling down upon the space which but an instant before had been crowded with workmen.' In a moment the earthquake had undone 'all that it had taken the garrison of Jalalabad three months to accomplish. The whole of the parapets which had been with so much skill and diligence constructed were thrown down with a fearful crash into heaps of ruins. In the walls, breaches were made, more accessible than any which the troops found when they first entered the place; and the entire circuit was more or less shaken. As to the houses in the town, there was scarcely one of them which escaped more or less of damage. Some fell in altogether; others had their fronts or flanks destroyed and the roofs shaken down; and the cloud of dust which rose immediately on the occurrence of the catastrophe is described as having been portentous. Happily, very few lives were lost. By far the greater number of the troops, being without the walls when the shock came, stood upon the glacis, or lay flat, while it heaved beneath them, to witness the overthrow; and the guards, making for open spaces, escaped. Some natives were overwhelmed in the ruins of the houses where they sojourned; and

Colonel Monteith, before he could escape from the rampart, sustained some bruises. But, on the whole, the casualties were wonderfully rare ; and the stores, both of ammunition and salted provisions, sustained no damage.'

" Nothing could better exhibit the wholesome respect inspired by the attitude of the garrison than the neglect of Akbar Khan to seize this moment for assaulting the place. The opportunity was soon lost. On the morrow the pickaxes and spades of the indefatigable garrison were again busily at work. Grass-cutting and foraging parties still went forth daily, sustaining occasionally losses from the attacks of the enemy's cavalry, but always repulsing their assailants, and rarely returning empty-handed. The rifle was not at that time the trusty friend of the English soldier which it has since become, but the whole country within long range of the walls had been so carefully measured, and the practice had been so effective that every shot thrown where a group of Afghans assembled told. To such perfection, indeed, was the art of gunnery carried by the besieged, that it is stated that on one occasion Captain Backhouse struck down a single horseman more than a mile distant from the fort. As the month wore on, the Afghan investment became closer, and the harassment of their fire more galling to the working parties and the men on the ramparts. On the 2nd of March, towards evening, a party of sappers sallied forth and drove the enemy's skirmishers away. The Afghans were continuously receiving reinforcements, but the besieged, though compelled to husband their failing stock of ammunition, made many successful sorties, and the attempts to interfere with the foraging parties were rarely completely successful. On one occasion a party of cavalry and infantry, suddenly issuing from the gates, boldly marched down upon the flocks of the enemy, and, before they could be interfered with, actually returned into the town, driving before them not fewer than 500 head of sheep. Both food and ammunition, however, began at last to fail. For upwards of four months the garrison had thus maintained itself isolated in the heart of an enemy's country; the time had come when more decisive steps must be taken. It was now the 7th of April, and instead of the deep snows and bitter frosts which the forces under General Elphinstone had to encounter, the weather was fine and favourable for military operations. The army was, moreover, in comparatively good condition—inured to hard work and harder fighting, and too well accustomed to take the measure of their enemy to be daunted by his greatly superior numbers. On that day was fought the memorable battle outside the walls of Jalalabad. Some of the most valuable officers in the army of the Indus fell in that obstinately-contested struggle, but the result was a victory which could not have been more complete. Camp baggage, artillery, standards, horses, and arms of every kind fell into our hands, together with abundant ammunition. The redoubtable Akbar fled towards Cabul with the wreck of his army; and in one day the besieged in Jalalabad, who had been put on half-rations, found themselves in possession of abundance of provisions. The tide had already turned; and it is important to observe that all this was achieved before the arrival of any succour from without. What more conclusive evidence could be furnished of the melancholy truth that the overwhelming disasters of the Koord Cabul were literally of our own seeking? Who can reasonably doubt that what Sale had done at Jalalabad, Elphinstone, or some commander less enfeebled by ill-health, could have accomplished at Cabul? To meet death fighting in the cantonments, or within the strong walls of the Bala Hissar, would at least have been preferable to the tender mercies of the Afghans and the rigours of a winter in the rugged and tortuous passes of the White Mountains; but, with unaccountable infatuation, the efforts to obtain supplies had been delayed at Cabul until even the means of equipping foraging parties were wanting.

"On the morrow of that battle a market was actually opened outside the gates of Jalalabad, to which the country people brought their wares to be exchanged for the coin of the Feringhees. On the 10th, Pollock's army was heard of as having reached the middle of the Khaibar. The difficulties of the Pass, in spite of the resistance of the Afreedis, who had seized the fort of Ali Musjid, had all been surmounted with the loss of only one officer killed, two or three wounded, and about 135 men killed and wounded. On the 16th, Pollock's column marched into the beleaguered city, accompanied by the bands of the garrison regiments, who had come forth to meet them, and who greeted them, as Mr. Gleig tells us, with the old Jacobite melody, 'Oh, but ye've been lang a comin'.' The forward movement upon Cabul, however, was not begun until August. Wave after wave of the troops despatched to Afghanistan arrived, until the entire force, consisting of nine or ten thousand well-disciplined troops, attended by five or six thousand Sikh soldiers, and the enormous number of 40,000 camp followers, were ready to march. In the fatal passes of Jugdulluck and the Koord Cabul they found the bleached bones of their unfortunate comrades. Preparations had been made by the Ghilzyes to oppose our advance; but our troops swept the heights, and their resistance was overcome with but trifling losses. In the valley of the Tezeen, where so many of General Elphinstone's army had fallen, Akbar Khan made a last stand, but was defeated with scarcely more sacrifice of life on our side. Similar successes attended General Nott's advance in Western Afghanistan. Ghazni was retaken with little difficulty, the march continued triumphantly on both sides, and on the 17th September the combined forces re-entered Cabul. In brief, the second invasion of Afghanistan by a comparatively small English army had been accomplished with scarcely more difficulty than the first. Only three days later the brave Sale had the happiness of regaining his long-lost wife, together with his daughter, Mrs. Sturt, whose husband had fallen in the disastrous retreat. The prisoners had, on the whole, been kindly treated, though their privations, hurried as they had been about the country, and frequently removed from place to place, had necessarily been considerable; and Akbar, embittered by his defeats, had at last threatened to make presents of them to the chiefs of the barbarous tribes of Turkestan. Their release was ultimately obtained by bribing the Khan in charge of the fort at Bamecan, to whose custody Akbar had confided them. The total list of prisoners released on General Pollock's arrival at Cabul, as given in the appendix to Lieutenant Eyre's Journal, comprise thirty-six officers, nine ladies, twenty-one children, and fifty-five privates and other persons."

www.ingramcontent.com/pod-product-compliance
Lightning Source LLC
Chambersburg PA
CBHW031339230426
43670CB00006B/386